Get Ready!

FOR STANDARDIZED TESTS

GRADE THREE

Other Books in the *Get Ready!* Series:

Get Ready! for Standardized Tests: Grade 1 by Joseph Harris, Ph.D.

Get Ready! for Standardized Tests: Grade 2 by Joseph Harris, Ph.D.

Get Ready! for Standardized Tests: Grade 4 by Joseph Harris, Ph.D.

Get Ready! for Standardized Tests: Grade 5 by Leslie E. Talbott, Ph.D.

Get Ready! for Standardized Tests: Grade 6 by Shirley Vickery, Ph.D.

Get Ready!

FOR STANDARDIZED TESTS

GRADE THREE 3

Karen Mersky, Ph.D.

Carol Turkington
Series Editor

McGraw-Hill

New York   San Francisco   Washington, D.C.   Auckland   Bogotá
Caracas   Lisbon   London   Madrid   Mexico City   Milan
Montreal   New Delhi   San Juan   Singapore
Sydney   Tokyo   Toronto

Library of Congress Cataloging-in-Publication Data

Get ready! for standardized tests / c Carol Turkington, series editor.
    p. cm.
    Includes bibliographical references.
    Contents: [1] Grade 1 / Joseph Harris — [2] Grade 2 / Joseph Harris — [3] Grade 3 / Karen Mersky — [4] Grade 4 / Joseph Harris — [5] Grade 5 / Leslie E. Talbott — [6] Grade 6 / Shirley Vickery.
    ISBN 0-07-136010-7 (v. 1) — ISBN 0-07-136011-5 (v. 2) — ISBN 0-07-136012-3 (v. 3) — ISBN 0-07-136013-1 (v. 4) — ISBN 0-07-136014-X (v. 5) — ISBN 0-07-136015-8 (v. 6)
    1. Achievement tests—United States—Study guides.   2. Education, Elementary—United States—Evaluation.   3. Education, Elementary—Parent participation—United States.   I. Turkington, Carol.   II. Harris, Joseph.

LB3060.22 .G48   2000
372.126—dc21

00-056083

McGraw-Hill

A Division of The McGraw-Hill Companies

1 2 3 4 5 6 7 8 9 0 PBT/PBT 0 9 8 7 6 5 4 3 2 1 0

ISBN 0-07-136012-3

This book was set in New Century Schoolbook by Inkwell Publishing Services.

Printed and bound by Phoenix Book Technology.

McGraw-Hill books are available at special quantity discounts to use as premiums and sales promotions, or for use in corporate training programs. For more information, please write to the Director of Special Sales, McGraw-Hill, Professional Publishing, Two Penn Plaza, New York, NY 10121-2298. Or contact your local bookstore.

To my wonderful family, without whose patience and support I could not have accomplished this project. Thank you for giving me those many "I'll be with you in a minute" moments in front of the computer!

I also wish to acknowledge the many fine teachers with whom I have had the opportunity to work over the years. The ideas and activities presented in this book are the result of these alliances, as together we have sought to enhance the education and learning of students.

Contents

Skills Checklist   ix

Introduction   1

Types of Standardized Tests   1
The Major Standardized Tests   2
How States Use Standardized Tests   2
Valid Uses of Standardized Test Scores   3
Inappropriate Use of Standardized
  Test Scores   3
Two Basic Assumptions   4
A Word about Coaching   4
How to Raise Test Scores   4
Test Questions   5

Chapter 1. Test-Taking Basics   7

The Purpose of This Book   7
The Third-Grade Student   8
How to Help Your Child   9
A Final Word   11

Chapter 2. Word Analysis   13

What Your Third Grader Should Be
  Learning   13
What Tests May Ask   13
What You and Your Child Can Do   13
Letters and Their Sounds   14
Hearing Similarities in Sounds   15
Word Study   15
What You Can Do   16
Practice Skill: Word Analysis   18

Chapter 3. Vocabulary   21

What Your Third Grader Should Be
  Learning   21
What Tests May Ask   21
Word Meanings   22
What You and Your Child Can Do   22
Words in Context   24
What You and Your Child Can Do   25
Practice Skill: Vocabulary   26

**Chapter 4. Reading
Comprehension**   31

What Your Third Grader Should Be
  Learning   31
What Tests May Ask   31
Inferential Comprehension   32
Critical Reading   32
What You and Your Child Can Do   33
Types of Reading   34
Study Skills   34
Alphabetizing   34
Dictionary Skills   34
What You and Your Child Can Do   35
Practice Skill: Reading Comprehension   35

**Chapter 5. Language
Mechanics**   39

What Your Third Grader Should Be
  Learning   39
What Tests May Ask   39

Capitalization 39
Punctuation 39
Sentence Structure 40
Word Usage: Pronouns 40
Spelling 40
What You and Your Child Can Do 41
Practice Skill: Capitalization and
  Punctuation 42
Practice Skill: Sentence Structure 43
Practice Skill: Word Usage 43

Chapter 6. Math Concepts 47

What Your Third Grader Should Be
  Learning 47
Sequence 47
Place Value 47
Reading Numbers 48
Numbers in Word Form 48
Expanded Form 48
Writing from Words 48
Manipulatives 48
Properties 48
What You and Your Child Can Do 49
Practice Skill: Math Concepts 50

Chapter 7. Math Computation 53

What Your Third Grader Should Be
  Learning 53
What Tests May Ask 53
Addition 53
Regrouping 54
Practice Skill: Addition 55
Subtraction 56
Mixing Problems 57
Practice Skill: Subtraction 58
Multiplication 58
Practice Skill: Multiplication 59
Division 60
What You and Your Child Can Do 60
Practice Skill: Division 61

Chapter 8. Math Applications 63

What Your Third Grader Should Be
  Learning 63
What Tests May Ask 63
Time 63
What You and Your Child Can Do 63
Money 64
What You and Your Child Can Do 64
Fractions 65
What You and Your Child Can Do 65
Interpreting Data 65
What You and Your Child Can Do 66
Geometry 66
What You and Your Child Can Do 67
Word Problems 67
What You and Your Child Can Do 68
Challenge Word Problems 68
Practice Skill: Math Applications 69

Appendix A: Web Sites and Resources for More Information 71

Appendix B: Read More about It 75

Appendix C: What Your Child's Test Scores Mean 77

Appendix D: Which States Require Which Tests 85

Appendix E: Testing Accommodations 95

Glossary 97

Answer Keys for Practice Skills 99

Sample Practice Test 101

Answer Key for Sample Practice Test 121

SKILLS CHECKLIST

MY CHILD ...	HAS LEARNED	IS WORKING ON
WORD ANALYSIS		
Phonics		
Prefixes and suffixes		
Compound words		
Contractions		
VOCABULARY		
Definitions (alone and in context)		
Synonyms		
Antonyms		
Multi-meaning words		
READING COMPREHENSION		
Fact recall		
Sequencing		
Cause and effect		
Main idea		
Making inferences		
Fact vs. opinion		
Fantasy vs. reality		
Fiction vs. nonfiction		
Alphabetizing		
Dictionary use		
LANGUAGE MECHANICS		
Capitalization		
Punctuation		
Spelling		
Homonyms		
Word usage		
MATH CONCEPTS		
Place value		
Sequences		
Comparisons		
Properties		
MATH COMPUTATION		
Addition		
Subtraction		
Multiplication		
Division		
Multi-digit computation		
Regrouping		
MATH APPLICATIONS		
Time		
Money		
Fractions		
Interpreting data		
Measurement		
Shapes and their properties		
Perimeter		
Word problems		

Introduction

Almost all of us have taken standardized tests in school. We spent several days bubbling-in answers, shifting in our seats. No one ever told us why we took the tests or what they would do with the results. We just took them and never heard about them again.

Today many parents aren't aware they are entitled to see their children's permanent records and, at a reasonable cost, to obtain copies of any information not protected by copyright, including testing scores. Late in the school year, most parents receive standardized test results with confusing bar charts and detailed explanations of scores that few people seem to understand.

In response to a series of negative reports on the state of education in this country, Americans have begun to demand that something be done to improve our schools. We have come to expect higher levels of accountability as schools face the competing pressures of rising educational expectations and declining school budgets. High-stakes standardized tests are rapidly becoming the main tool of accountability for students, teachers, and school administrators. If students' test scores don't continually rise, teachers and principals face the potential loss of school funding and, ultimately, their jobs. Summer school and private after-school tutorial program enrollments are swelling with students who have not met score standards or who, everyone agrees, could score higher.

While there is a great deal of controversy about whether it is appropriate for schools to use standardized tests to make major decisions about individual students, it appears likely that standardized tests are here to stay. They will be used to evaluate students, teachers, and the schools; schools are sure to continue to use students' test scores to demonstrate their accountability to the community.

The purposes of this guide are to acquaint you with the types of standardized tests your children may take; to help you understand the test results; and to help you work with your children in skill areas that are measured by standardized tests so they can perform as well as possible.

Types of Standardized Tests

The two major types of group standardized tests are *criterion-referenced tests* and *norm-referenced tests*. Think back to when you learned to tie your shoes. First Mom or Dad showed you how to loosen the laces on your shoe so that you could insert your foot; then they showed you how to tighten the laces—but not too tight. They showed you how to make bows and how to tie a knot. All the steps we just described constitute what is called a *skills hierarchy:* a list of skills from easiest to most difficult that are related to some goal, such as tying a shoelace.

Criterion-referenced tests are designed to determine at what level students are performing on various skills hierarchies. These tests assume that development of skills follows a sequence of steps. For example, if you were teaching shoelace tying, the skills hierarchy might appear this way:

1. Loosen laces.
2. Insert foot.
3. Tighten laces.
4. Make loops with both lace ends.
5. Tie a square knot.

Criterion-referenced tests try to identify how far along the skills hierarchy the student has progressed. There is no comparison against any-one else's score, only against an expected skill level. The main question criterion-referenced tests ask is: "Where is this child in the development of this group of skills?"

Norm-referenced tests, in contrast, are typically constructed to compare children in their abilities as to different skills areas. Although the experts who design test items may be aware of skills hierarchies, they are more concerned with how much of some skill the child has mastered, rather than at what level on the skills hierarchy the child is.

Ideally, the questions on these tests range from very easy items to those that are impossibly difficult. The essential feature of norm-referenced tests is that scores on these measures can be compared to scores of children in similar groups. They answer this question: "How does the child compare with other children of the same age or grade placement in the development of this skill?"

This book provides strategies for increasing your child's scores on both standardized norm-referenced and criterion-referenced tests.

The Major Standardized Tests

Many criterion-referenced tests currently in use are created locally or (at best) on a state level,

and there are far too many of them to go into detail here about specific tests. However, children prepare for them in basically the same way they do for norm-referenced tests.

A very small pool of norm-referenced tests is used throughout the country, consisting primarily of the Big Five:

- California Achievement Tests (CTB/McGraw-Hill)
- Iowa Tests of Basic Skills (Riverside)
- Metropolitan Achievement Test (Harcourt-Brace & Company)
- Stanford Achievement Test (Psychological Corporation)
- TerraNova [formerly Comprehensive Test of Basic Skills] (McGraw-Hill)

These tests use various terms for the academic skills areas they assess, but they generally test several types of reading, language, and mathematics skills, along with social studies and science. They may include additional assessments, such as of study and reference skills.

How States Use Standardized Tests

Despite widespread belief and practice to the contrary, group standardized tests are designed to assess and compare the achievement of groups. They are *not* designed to provide detailed diagnostic assessments of individual students. (For detailed individual assessments, children should be given individual diagnostic tests by properly qualified professionals, including trained guidance counselors, speech and language therapists, and school psychologists.) Here are examples of the types of questions group standardized tests are designed to answer:

- How did the reading achievement of students at Valley Elementary School this year compare with their reading achievement last year?

- How did math scores at Wonderland Middle School compare with those of students at Parkside Middle School this year?

- As a group, how did Hilltop High School students compare with the national averages in the achievement areas tested?

- How did the district's first graders' math scores compare with the district's fifth graders' math scores?

The fact that these tests are designed primarily to test and compare groups doesn't mean that test data on individual students isn't useful. It does mean that when we use these tests to diagnose individual students, we are using them for a purpose for which they were not designed.

Think of group standardized tests as being similar to health fairs at the local mall. Rather than check into your local hospital and spend thousands of dollars on full, individual tests for a wide range of conditions, you can go from station to station and take part in different health screenings. Of course, one would never diagnose heart disease or cancer on the basis of the screening done at the mall. At most, suspicious results on the screening would suggest that you need to visit a doctor for a more complete examination.

In the same way, group standardized tests provide a way of screening the achievement of many students quickly. Although you shouldn't diagnose learning problems solely based on the results of these tests, the results can tell you that you should think about referring a child for a more definitive, individual assessment.

An individual student's group test data should be considered only a point of information. Teachers and school administrators may use standardized test results to support or question hypotheses they have made about students; but these scores must be used alongside other information, such as teacher comments, daily work, homework, class test grades, parent observations, medical needs, and social history.

Valid Uses of Standardized Test Scores

Here are examples of appropriate uses of test scores for individual students:

- Mr. Cone thinks that Samantha, a third grader, is struggling in math. He reviews her file and finds that her first- and second-grade standardized test math scores were very low. Her first- and second-grade teachers recall episodes in which Samantha cried because she couldn't understand certain math concepts, and mention that she was teased by other children, who called her "Dummy." Mr. Cone decides to refer Samantha to the school assistance team to determine whether she should be referred for individual testing for a learning disability related to math.

- The local college wants to set up a tutoring program for elementary school children who are struggling academically. In deciding which youngsters to nominate for the program, the teachers consider the students' averages in different subjects, the degree to which students seem to be struggling, parents' reports, and standardized test scores.

- For the second year in a row, Gene has performed poorly on the latest round of standardized tests. His teachers all agree that Gene seems to have some serious learning problems. They had hoped that Gene was immature for his class and that he would do better this year; but his dismal grades continue. Gene is referred to the school assistance team to determine whether he should be sent to the school psychologist for assessment of a possible learning handicap.

Inappropriate Use of Standardized Test Scores

Here are examples of how schools have sometimes used standardized test results inappropriately:

- Mr. Johnson groups his students into reading groups solely on the basis of their standardized test scores.

- Ms. Henry recommends that Susie be held back a year because she performed poorly on the standardized tests, despite strong grades on daily assignments, homework, and class tests.

- Gerald's teacher refers him for consideration in the district's gifted program, which accepts students using a combination of intelligence test scores, achievement test scores, and teacher recommendations. Gerald's intelligence test scores were very high. Unfortunately, he had a bad cold during the week of the standardized group achievement tests and was taking powerful antihistamines, which made him feel sleepy. As a result, he scored too low on the achievement tests to qualify.

The public has come to demand increasingly high levels of accountability for public schools. We demand that schools test so that we have hard data with which to hold the schools accountable. But too often, politicians and the public place more faith in the test results than is justified. Regardless of whether it's appropriate to do so and regardless of the reasons schools use standardized test results as they do, many schools base crucial programming and eligibility decisions on scores from group standardized tests. It's to your child's advantage, then, to perform as well as possible on these tests.

Two Basic Assumptions

The strategies we present in this book come from two basic assumptions:

1. Most students can raise their standardized test scores.

2. Parents can help their children become stronger in the skills the tests assess.

This book provides the information you need to learn what skill areas the tests measure, what general skills your child is being taught in a particular grade, how to prepare your child to take the tests, and what to do with the results. In the appendices you will find information to help you decipher test interpretations; a listing of which states currently require what tests; and additional resources to help you help your child to do better in school and to prepare for the tests.

A Word about Coaching

This guide is *not* about coaching your child. When we use the term *coaching* in referring to standardized testing, we mean trying to give someone an unfair advantage, either by revealing beforehand what exact items will be on the test or by teaching "tricks" that will supposedly allow a student to take advantage of some detail in how the tests are constructed.

Some people try to coach students in shrewd test-taking strategies that take advantage of how the tests are supposedly constructed rather than strengthening the students' skills in the areas tested. Over the years, for example, many rumors have been floated about "secret formulas" that test companies use.

This type of coaching emphasizes ways to help students obtain scores they didn't earn—to get something for nothing. Stories have appeared in the press about teachers who have coached their students on specific questions, parents who have tried to obtain advance copies of tests, and students who have written down test questions after taking standardized tests and sold them to others. Because of the importance of test security, test companies and states aggressively prosecute those who attempt to violate test security—and they should do so.

How to Raise Test Scores

Factors that are unrelated to how strong students are but that might artificially lower test scores include anything that prevents students from making scores that accurately describe their actual abilities. Some of those factors are:

- giving the tests in uncomfortably cold or hot rooms;

- allowing outside noises to interfere with test taking; and

- reproducing test booklets in such small print or with such faint ink that students can't read the questions.

Such problems require administrative attention from both the test publishers, who must make sure that they obtain their norms for the tests under the same conditions students face when they take the tests; and school administrators, who must ensure that conditions under which their students take the tests are as close as possible to those specified by the test publishers.

Individual students also face problems that can artificially lower their test scores, and parents can do something about many of these problems. Stomach aches, headaches, sleep deprivation, colds and flu, and emotional upsets due to a recent tragedy are problems that might call for the student to take the tests during make-up sessions. Some students have physical conditions such as muscle-control problems, palsies, or difficulty paying attention that require work over many months or even years before students can obtain accurate test scores on standardized tests. And, of course, some students just don't take the testing seriously or may even intentionally perform poorly. Parents can help their children overcome many of these obstacles to obtaining accurate scores.

Finally, with this book parents are able to help their children raise their scores by:

- increasing their familiarity (and their comfort level) with the types of questions on standardized tests;

- drills and practice exercises to increase their skill in handling the kinds of questions they will meet; and

- providing lots of fun ways for parents to help their children work on the skill areas that will be tested.

Test Questions

The favorite type of question for standardized tests is the multiple-choice question. For example:

1. The first President of the United States was:

   A Abraham Lincoln

   B Martin Luther King, Jr.

   C George Washington

   D Thomas Jefferson

The main advantage of multiple-choice questions is that it is easy to score them quickly and accurately. They lend themselves to optical scanning test forms, on which students fill in bubbles or squares and the forms are scored by machine. Increasingly, companies are moving from paper-based testing to computer-based testing, using multiple-choice questions.

The main disadvantage of multiple-choice questions is that they restrict test items to those that can be put in that form. Many educators and civil rights advocates have noted that the multiple-choice format only reveals a superficial understanding of the subject. It's not possible with multiple-choice questions to test a student's ability to construct a detailed, logical argument on some issue or to explain a detailed process. Although some of the major tests are beginning to incorporate more subjectively scored items, such as short answer or essay questions, the vast majority of test items continue to be in multiple-choice format.

In the past, some people believed there were special formulas or tricks to help test-takers determine which multiple-choice answer was the correct one. There may have been some truth to *some* claims for past tests. Computer analyses of some past tests revealed certain biases in how tests were constructed. For example, the old advice to pick *D* when in doubt appears to have been valid for some past tests. However, test publishers have become so sophisticated in their ability to detect patterns of bias in the formulation of test questions and answers that they now guard against it aggressively.

In Chapter 1, we provide information about general test-taking considerations, with advice on how parents can help students overcome testing obstacles. The rest of the book provides information to help parents help their children strengthen skills in the tested areas.

Joseph Harris, Ph.D.

Test-Taking Basics

As part of their educational careers, almost all children must take a series of standardized tests. During the early years, these tests can be very helpful in ensuring that your child is learning to the best of his or her ability. Standardized tests aren't designed to be pass or fail, but rather to show a student's areas of strength and areas that may need further development. This knowledge can be very useful to you and to your child's teacher. In the school setting, skills often build on each other; if educational needs are identified as they emerge, a child is less likely to become frustrated or feel that learning is an overwhelming project. In addition, ignoring an early gap in learning can lead to repeated failure. By using the results of standardized tests in an informed way, you can help give your child the best possible educational experience.

Standardized tests can be useful, but it's also important to remember that they provide only one measure of a child's work. Many factors can affect a child's performance, only one of which is difficulty mastering the material. A child who is feeling ill, hungry, or tired is less likely to have the stamina for maintaining good focus. This might cause the child to miss one of the question spaces on the answer sheet, which will throw off all subsequent answers.

Similarly, some children are particularly anxious during tests; worrying leaves less energy and thinking power for answering the questions, even though the child may know how to do the problem. Therefore, in order to understand the full significance of your child's scores, it's important to integrate them with information about your child's classroom performance. Then any discrepancies can be explained in a more meaningful way.

The Purpose of This Book

This book is designed to familiarize you with the skills taught in a typical third-grade classroom. If you understand what your child is expected to learn, you will be in a better position to work with your child's teacher. Educators believe that the most effective educational system is one in which parents and the school work together. The activities and suggestions in this book **are *not*** meant to take the place of your child's teacher. It is important to remember that learning is an ongoing process. Time and practice can often be keys to success. Therefore, your reinforcing what is being taught in the classroom can be very helpful for your child.

Before getting into specific strategies to help your child, it's important to discuss how these strategies should be used. Most children want to do well. However, they spend many hours at school and often have daily homework to complete when they arrive home. In addition, many children are involved in organized activities outside of school. Additional educational activities such as the ones suggested here should not become all-encompassing; children need time to use their imaginations and to develop their own forms of play.

When you carry out these activities, *make them fun.* You can be the student and your child can be the teacher. Explaining something to someone or checking what she did can be just as effective a learning tool as doing it yourself. So be the student, but make mistakes and have your child try to catch them.

Be creative as you work on the skills. Look around you for real-world examples of the skills you are practicing. Information that is integrated into a meaningful framework is often easier to recall than that which is learned in isolation. Remember from your own school days when learning interesting subjects was easier than learning less interesting subjects? Most likely, the subjects you found interesting were the ones that were more meaningful to you.

Another important key to success is to make sure your child doesn't do too much at one time. Taking smaller, successful steps can be more effective than taking a giant step with lots of falling down. Your child should spend no more than about 20 minutes at a time on these activities, tempered by the amount of homework your child has for the day and any other outside commitments that have been scheduled (such as sports, religious classes, music lessons, or medical appointments). In order to avoid a time crunch, try to start these activities early; if you can, start when school begins in September. That way you can follow what the teacher is doing to help ensure that your child is mastering what is presented in class. Working over a longer period of time also makes the work less stressful for you and your child. It gives you lots of time to praise and encourage your child. Developing confidence goes a long way toward helping a child be successful!

If your child resists your efforts, or you're feeling frustrated with your child's success in learning a skill presented in this book, stop the work and try to figure out what's happening. Is the time fun? Are the activities creative and inter-esting? What is competing for your child's attention? How long have you been working? If these factors don't point to the problem, discuss your concerns with your child's teacher. If your child is having similar problems at school, your teacher will be able to help you find out what the problem is. This book will not have served its purpose if all it does is create conflict and frustration.

No book can cover every possible type of question on all standardized tests, nor can your child be expected to answer every question he may encounter. These tests are designed to include challenging questions for many of the students who take them. In addition, not all third-grade classes cover the same material. While there is certainly an overlap, the exact curriculum varies from one school to the next. The purpose of this book is to help you make sure your child understands the major concepts typical of a third-grade curriculum that are likely to be presented on a standardized test.

The Third-Grade Student

As your child turns 8, he or she enters what psy-chologists refer to as *middle childhood.* Children in this stage of development become better able to think flexibly and independently and, therefore, become ready for more advanced concepts within the curriculum. For example, when presented with several groups of objects, a third grader can understand that both quanti-ties may be the same, despite differences in appearance. Children in middle childhood are less likely to be deceived by misleading physical cues. In addition, children at this stage begin to be able to shift their perspective so that a change in one dimension is understood as being compensated for by a change in another dimen-sion. In other words, they understand that a tall, thin vase may hold the same amount of water as a short, fatter vase.

Between the ages of 6 and 9, children gradu-ally develop the capacity to perform mental operations. Being able to do things in their head, they can compare two sets of items, one of which includes the other. For example, children can now answer the question, "Are there more red flowers or flowers?" "Flowers" is a larger set, of which the red flowers are only one subset.

Similarly, children this age can begin to think of elements that could belong to several categories at the same time. As a result of these changes in thinking skills, the curriculum becomes less tied to physical, concrete learning. Your child is entering the stage when she can grasp both concepts and the relationships between concepts. During this stage of development, children also become better able to understand the perspective of another person, while becoming more certain of their own responses; the group no longer sways them as it did before. At the same time, children at this age are becoming more adept at language. They are better at understanding the multiple meanings of words and are learning to apply logic without having to tie it to a concrete object or a specific content. They become better at remembering, which enhances the ability to summarize information and develop ways of classifying things. All of these changes are reflected in the curriculum.

How to Help Your Child

Your child will likely do better on standardized tests if she understands what to expect and can listen and follow directions. A child who doesn't understand the directions or who is unfamiliar with the test format may not perform to the best of her ability. Therefore, it's important to prepare your child for the logistics of the testing situation.

Explain to your child that she'll be asked to complete booklets in school to help find out what she has learned so far. Let your child know that this process will be different than other school days, because the classroom will likely be particularly quiet and the teacher won't be able to help with the harder questions.

Most standardized tests for this age are designed so that the directions are read to the class, with sample questions completed as a group before the class formally begins each section. After the sample questions are given, your child will be responsible for reading each individual question and for reading the response choices. Let your child know that a practice question will be given and, if she doesn't understand what to do, it will be okay to ask the teacher to clarify the directions. (*Note:* The teacher may not be able to explain *why* the answer in the sample question is correct.)

Prepare your child for the broad nature of the tests. Let her know that some of the questions will be easier than others. **But even on the difficult questions, it will be important for your child to think about each choice before answering and to try to do her best.** As you work with your child, remember that this book covers a great deal of curriculum information. All children don't learn skills at the same pace; we all do some things better than others. In addition, standardized tests can't include questions to assess every skill. Therefore, there will likely be only a few questions for each of the skills discussed in this book. This means that if your child isn't 100 percent proficient in mastering place value, for example, his overall performance on the Math Concepts section may not necessarily be poor.

Using a multiple-choice format, most standardized tests require students to fill in a small bubble near the correct answer. You'll find a sample test at the end of this chapter (Sample Test A). If your child has difficulty with the format, make up your own sample test. Put in some easy questions to familiarize your child with the format, then include more difficult ones to help impress upon him that he needs to work carefully.

It's important that your child **listen very carefully** during the directions and during the reading of the questions. Some questions will be worded in a less obvious way: Which does *not* belong? Which could *not* happen? You can help your child by playing listening games, including memory games such as these two:

1. *I'm going on a vacation and I'm going to take....*" The first person repeats the sentence and then adds an item. For each remaining turn, the person repeats the sentence beginning and lists all the previously stated items, then adds another item.

    YOU: I'm going on vacation and I'm going to take a baseball.

    CHILD: I'm going on vacation and I'm going to take a baseball and a book.

    As the list grows, it gets harder to recall the items and to do so in order. Playing games such as this helps to develop listening skills and auditory memory.

2. *Giving instructions.* Give your child sets of directions as you go through your typical day. Instead of telling your child to do one thing at a time, ask that he *brush* his teeth, *put* his clothes in the hamper, and *get* a book to read. You can make requests fun by throwing in tricks. *"You need to go hang up your coat and if you sing a song, we can have some ice cream for dessert tonight,"* or *"If you sing a song, we can play a game of UNO."* Don't give the ice cream or play UNO unless your child heard you the first time. If he asks "What?," tell him to try again next time.

A sample test that focuses on following directions is included at the end of this chapter (Sample Test B). Remind your child to read directions carefully and not take anything for granted. It's easy for children to assume that they know what to do. Help your child learn the following tips:

• Do what the directions say, not what you think they mean.

• Concentrate and reread the directions if you need to.

• Ask a question if you don't understand what to do.

In addition to helping your child develop good listening skills, notice the kind of mistakes she makes as you work on the material presented in this book. Looking at mistakes can be a very productive way of understanding how a child is thinking, so that instruction can be made more effective. For example, look at the following incorrect answers:

Find a word with the same vowel sound as <u>weigh</u>.

<u>receive</u>   boat   same   beg

Find a word with the same vowel sound as <u>beam</u>.

meet   said   <u>head</u>   build

In each case, the child chose the wrong response, but the pattern in the errors suggest that the child is looking at the letters within the words and not listening to how the words sound.

It's important for your child to work carefully and to consider all choices before choosing the correct one. Often this involves reciting the question with each response choice to see which is best. In the above examples, the child would say to herself:

weigh	receive
weigh	boat
weigh	same
weigh	beg

If your child is unsure of an answer, have him eliminate the ones he knows are incorrect. This gives him better odds of choosing the correct response.

Look at your child's papers from school. Does he follow directions carefully, or are parts omitted? Assess how your child follows directions at home. Do all of the steps get followed carefully, or are parts forgotten? Does she ask for clarification when needed?

The tips presented here can be used for all

schoolwork, not just for standardized tests; they're just good study habits. The night before your child is tested, make sure she gets a good night's sleep. Equally important, make sure she eats a healthy breakfast each morning. These are easy ways to reduce the artificial factors that can affect a child's score.

As you work through this book, you will find many different activities to do with your child. If a particular activity is especially enjoyable, feel free to adapt it to any of the other concepts. All children don't enjoy the same types of activities, and only you know your child best. If your child's teacher has presented a particular activity that your child enjoys, use that to reinforce the concepts, adapting it as possible. Remember that it's not necessary to complete this book from start to finish. Perhaps your child enjoys doing more difficult things first. Another child might benefit from having extra practice with math, because he's not as strong in that subject. He may want to start with the math chapters so there is extra time to review. A checklist is provided at the beginning of this book so you can keep track of the areas you work on, regardless of the order in which you do so.

A Final Word

Not everything that is taught in third grade—or that could possibly be on a given standardized test—can be included in one book. Trying to teach "everything" to your child is an impossible task, and would require a book too lengthy to be practical. The information presented here should be used in conjunction with the work that your child is doing in school to help develop essential skills in reading, written expression, and mathematics.

Given that children learn academic concepts at different rates, and given that everyone has areas of strength and areas that are less developed, focus your attention on those skills that your child needs additional practice in, with periodic review of the other areas.

Sample questions are included with each chapter. These questions are designed to help familiarize your child with the types of questions that may be on a given standardized test. These questions are **not** a measure of your child's proficiency in any given content area; but if your child is having difficulty with a particular question, use that information to determine what skills she needs extra practice in.

From your own experience, you may remember that curriculum areas overlap. As a result, questions on a particular skill may be found in a different chapter than expected. For example, adding a verb ending is discussed in Chapter 2, Word Analysis, but questions on verb endings appear in Chapter 5: Language Mechanics. There is no set way you must work through this book. Instead, use it as a resource to help you work with your child.

Sample Test A

Directions: Choose the best answer to the following questions.

1 I am a
   (A) boy   (B) girl
   (C) man   (D) woman

2 I live in a
   (A) house   (B) apartment
   (C) trailer   (D) condominium

3 My favorite food is
   (A) pizza   (B) hot dog
   (C) ice cream   (D) tacos

4 Beanie Babies are
   (A) large   (B) hard
   (C) soft   (D) people

5 Which animal usually lives in a house?

Ⓐ cat Ⓑ elephant

Ⓒ rhinoceros Ⓓ giraffe

6 Which candy is smallest?

Ⓐ M&Ms Ⓑ Hershey Kiss

Ⓒ Snickers bar Ⓓ 3 Musketeers

7 Which instrument has strings?

Ⓐ flute Ⓑ drums

Ⓒ violin Ⓓ trumpet

8 What are you least likely to see in a park?

Ⓐ swings Ⓑ bench

Ⓒ trees Ⓓ cage

9 What could you wear on your feet?

Ⓐ gloves Ⓑ scarf

Ⓒ socks Ⓓ hat

10 Which would you be more likely to get at Halloween?

Ⓐ broccoli Ⓑ candy

Ⓒ carrot Ⓓ peach

11 Which are you least likely to find in the kitchen?

Ⓐ soup Ⓑ tub

Ⓒ milk Ⓓ hamburger

Sample Test B

Parent: Give your child a blank piece of paper. Then read the directions aloud.

Directions: Read all of the following questions carefully before you begin. You will have three minutes to complete this test. Ready; begin.

1 Put your name in the upper left-hand corner of the paper.

2 Put your telephone number in the lower right hand corner of the paper.

3 Draw two squares, one triangle, and one rectangle.

4 Put your address under your name.

5 Add 937 and 671.

6 Stand up and clap your hands two times.

7 Give two meanings of "fly."

8 Subtract 451 from 562.

9 Write a synonym for BIG.

10 Raise your hand and say "Sally sells seashells."

11 Write five words that rhyme with HAT.

12 Write the even numbers from 4 to 14.

13 Write the numbers from 20 to 10 backwards.

14 Now that you have read each question, answer only the first one. Then go play. Don't answer any other questions.

CHAPTER 2

Word Analysis

Word analysis refers to the composition of words—the fact that words are made up of letters, which represent sounds. This chapter first presents the letters and sounds that are often taught in third grade. The particular phonics rules associated with each of these are also presented. It's important for you to know these rules to help your child sound out words when reading as well as to help your child with spelling.

What Your Third Grader Should Be Learning

To become a good reader, your child needs to know how to be able to separate, manipulate, and identify the sounds that are within words and be able to specify the letters that make those sounds. In addition, your child needs to understand the structure of words—specifically, that words are composed of separate parts.

What Tests May Ask

The word analysis section of a standardized test assesses how well your child understands the composition of words and how well she can separate and identify word sounds and the letters that make up the sounds.

One way standardized tests assess your child's facility with word analysis is by asking your child to hear and identify similarities in words.

Which word begins the same as goat?

giant   game   jelly

Which word has the same vowel sound as beam?

meet   head   build

Your child may also be asked a straightforward identification question:

Which word is a compound word?

baseball   mistake   wonderful

What is the contraction for we will?

he'll   she's   we'll

What You and Your Child Can Do

For many children, memorizing the rules of phonics is a difficult task. We've included the rules here so you can become familiar with them. As you do the activities in this chapter with your child, use the phonics information to explain a particular skill.

Studying information in a meaningful context often makes it easier to learn than trying to learn the same information in isolation. In addition, it's important to remember that the English language has many exceptions. As you work through these rules, you may think of examples that do not fit. These just have to be learned as "quirks."

Letters and Their Sounds

CONSONANTS

1. **Single consonant:** One letter has one sound, except **c** and **g**, which have two sounds.

   Rule: When the letter **c** or **g** is followed by **e, i,** or **y**, the **c** or **g** usually has a soft sound:

ra**c**e	**c**ity	fan**c**y
pa**g**e	**g**iant	**g**ypsy

   Rule: When the letter **c** or **g** is followed by the vowels **a, o**, or **u,** the **c** or **g** usually has a hard sound:

gain	**g**um	**g**ot
cat	**c**ot	**c**ut

2. **Consonant digraph:** Two consonants together make one sound.

wh	**wh**en	
th	**th**is	**th**in *(Note that **th** has two sounds.)*
ch	**ch**eck	
sh	**sh**eep	
ck	bla**ck**	
kn	**kn**ow	

3. **Consonant blends:** Two or more consonants are next to each other, and the consonant sounds blend together but each sound is heard.

bl	**bl**ack
tr	**tr**ee
spr	**spr**ing
st	fa**st**
mp	la**mp**
sk	de**sk**

SHORT VOWELS

Rule: If a word or syllable has only one vowel and it comes between two consonants or at the beginning of a word, it is usually short.

c**a**t	s**e**t	m**i**tt
h**o**t	b**u**n	**a**nt	**i**t

LONG VOWELS

Rule: If a one-syllable word has two vowels, usually the first is long and the second is silent. A long vowel says its name.

1. **CVCe** (consonant, vowel, consonant, e): The e on the end is silent; the first vowel says its name.

cake	Pete	bike	tone	mule

2. **Vowel pair:** Two vowels together make one sound.

train		long **a**
meet	leaf	long **e**
pie		long **i**
coat	toe	long **o**
glue	fruit	long **u**
hay		**ay** says long **a**

3. **Vowel at the end of a word:** If a word or syllable has only one vowel that comes at the end of the word or syllable, the vowel is usually long.

me	go

4. **Vowel digraph:** Two vowels together can make either a long or a short sound, or can have a special sound all their own.

   school   book   *(Note that **oo** has two sounds.)*

   bread

   eight

5. **Diphthong:** Two vowels together can blend to make one sound.

cl**ou**d   **oi**l   t**oy**

6. **R-controlled vowels**

Rule: When a vowel is followed by an *r*, it has a sound that is neither short nor long.

b**ir**d   c**ar**   f**or**   f**er**n   b**ur**n

7. **Y as a vowel:** When **y** is the only vowel at the end of a syllable or at the end of a word that has only one syllable, **y** has the long **i** sound.

fl**y**   m**y**

When **y** is the only vowel at the end of a word having more than one syllable, **y** has the long **e** sound.

sill**y**   funn**y**

Hearing Similarities in Sounds

In addition to knowing what the letter–sound associations are, your child should be able to hear and manipulate sounds within words. Specifically, your child should be able to identify words that rhyme. These are words that have the same ending sounds; spelling does not have to be the same: •

could, should, wood

bell, tell, smell

meat, feet, treat

Word Study

A second way of analyzing words is to look at them in terms of their structure. A base (or "root") word is a word to which a prefix or a suffix can be added to form a new word.

1. Prefix. A prefix is a word part added to the beginning of a word to change the word's meaning:

dis-	not	**dis**pleased = not pleased
un-	not	**un**folded = not folded
mis-	not right	**mis**placed = not in the right place
re-	do again	**re**read = read again
de-	from	**de**part = go away from
ex-	out of or from	**ex**port = send out of

2. Suffix. A suffix is a word part added to the end of a word to change the meaning or the way the word is used:

plurals show more than one of the object.

cat**s**   bush**es**

Rule: To make a word plural,

If the word ends in a consonant, add **-s:**

cat = cats

If the word ends in **ss, ch, z**, or **sh**, add **-es:**

dish = dishes   dress = dresses

If the word ends in a **y**, change the **y** to an **i** and add **-es:**.

fairy = fairies

If the word ends in **f** or **fe**, change the **f** or **fe** to a **v** and add **-es:**.

knife = knives   wolf = wolves

Verb tenses tell when the action occurred.

-ed   Puts the action in the past.

jump**ed**   *I jumped yesterday.*

-ing Tells that the action is going on now.

Jump**ing**   *I am jumping on my bed.*

Comparisons are used to compare two or more objects.

-er -est   busy, bus**ier**, bus**iest**

I am busier than you are.

Other suffixes are used to indicate specific meanings.

-ful	full of	hope**ful**
-ness	a condition of	sick**ness**
-less	without	help**less**
-ly	in a specified manner	slow**ly**
-y	characterized by	funn**y**
-en	caused to be	whit**en**
-able	capable of	wash**able**

Rules: To add a suffix:

If the word ends in two consonants, add the suffix.

jum<u>p</u>**ing**

If the word has a short vowel and ends in a single consonant, double the consonant and add the suffix.

ho<u>p</u>**ping**

If the word ends in a **y**, and the suffix begins with a vowel, change the **y** to an **i** and add the suffix.

bus<u>y</u> = bus**ier**

If the word ends in a silent **e**, and the suffix begins with a vowel, drop the **e** before adding a suffix.

bak<u>e</u> = bak**ing**

3. Compound Words. A compound word is a word that is made up of two real words.

cardboard = card + board

4. Contractions. A contraction is two words made into one shorter word by omitting letters.

Most contractions follow the pattern of dropping letters from the second word.

do not = don't

I will = I'll

they have = they've

there is = there's

they are = they're

let us = let's

Other contractions are irregular.

will not = won't

cannot = can't

5. Syllables. A syllable is a unit of spoken language consisting of an uninterrupted utterance that forms either a word or part of a word.

one syllable	book
two syllables	butter
three syllables	banana

Your child should know how many syllables a word has. Although there are numerous rules for dividing words into syllables, the important concept for your child to know is that each syllable has one vowel sound; this will help your child determine how many syllables a word has.

3 vowel sounds = 3 syllables	b<u>a</u>-n<u>a</u>n-<u>a</u>
2 vowel sounds = 2 syllables	c<u>a</u>r-p<u>e</u>t
1 vowel sound = 1 syllable	b<u>e</u>d st<u>o</u>ne

What You Can Do

Now that you are familiar with the phonics rules, here are some activities to use with your child as a way to strengthen her skills. Many of these activities don't require a specific study time, but are good time fillers while you're waiting in line at the movies or grocery store or while you're driving in the car. As you work through the phonics rules, pay particular attention to your child's understanding of long and short vowels; it's important that these are learned well.

Play I'm Going on Vacation. In this game each person begins by stating the sentence prompt (*I'm going on vacation and I'm going to take …*), and then repeats all previously stated items before adding a new one of his or her own.

YOU: I'm going on vacation and I'm going to take a bell.

CHILD: I'm going on vacation and I'm going to take a bell and a bicycle.

This game can be modified to put structure on the type of words generated. For example, if you are practicing the **long a** sound, then each word must contain that sound: I'm going on vacation and I'm going to take a game, a manger, a baseball…. If you are practicing plurals, each item must be a plural: I'm going on vacation and I'm going to take bats, candles, dishes….

Note: The sentence prompt can be anything you would like:

I'm going to a baseball game and I'm going to take …

I'm going to my tree house and I'm going to take …

Make Up Silly Couplets. Pick a specified rule, then see how many words you can generate to complete the beginning of a sentence. Make them as silly as you want, as long as each chosen word fits the specified rule.

If you want to practice rhyming words, for example, try these couplets:

A cat sat on a …

A cat sat on a hat.

A cat sat on a vat.

A cat sat on a rat.

Make Up Silly Tongue Twisters. Pick a specified rule and make up a tongue twister using words that follow that rule. If you want to practice plurals with "es," try: *The dishes with wishes had glasses in boxes.*

Create a Challenge. Pick a rule to work on and challenge your child to think of as many examples as she can. Make the challenge fun and concrete. For example, hang a long piece of paper from the top of the refrigerator and see if your child can make a list of compound words that reaches to the ground. Or, try to think of all the words that need **-es** to make them plural. Write each example on a 3 × 5-inch card and see if you can string the cards all the way around the kitchen or your child's room.

As an extra way to reinforce this concept, use different colored markers. For example:

Compound Words: **home**work

Plurals: Use **green** if the word ends in a **y** that you change to **i**:

fair**ies**

Use **blue** if the word ends in **-ss, x, sh,** or **ch:**

dishes

Have your child give you a *challenge* question before she leaves for school, goes to bed, hears a story, and so on.

Play School. Have your child make up a worksheet for you to complete. Go over the rule first to make sure your child knows what to do. As you complete the worksheet, make some mistakes for your child to catch.

Read to Your Child. As you read, have your child follow along with you. Let her be a detective and find any examples of a specified rule in the section that you read.

Have Your Child Read. By hearing her read aloud, you have the opportunity to observe your child practicing sounding out unfamiliar words. As you observe your child, note the types of words she has trouble with, and use these for more focused practice in the activities outlined above.

Reading provides exposure to more words than a worksheet with a limited number of sample questions. Reading provides practice in applying the rules; a worksheet provides a focused opportunity for instruction.

Practice Skill: Word Analysis

Directions: Answer the following questions:

1   Which word has the same vowel sound as <u>seat</u>?

   Ⓐ head
   Ⓑ need
   Ⓒ best
   Ⓓ male

2   Which word begins with the same sound as <u>jelly</u>?

   Ⓐ giant
   Ⓑ game
   Ⓒ guess
   Ⓓ girl

3   Which word has the same vowel sound as <u>seam</u>?

   Ⓐ make
   Ⓑ bread
   Ⓒ beet
   Ⓓ open

4   Which word is a compound word?

   Ⓐ busiest
   Ⓑ sunshine
   Ⓒ happiness
   Ⓓ handier

5   What is the contraction for <u>he will</u>?

   Ⓐ he'll
   Ⓑ she's
   Ⓒ we'll
   Ⓓ hew'll

6   Which word has the same ending sound as <u>funny</u>?

   Ⓐ silly
   Ⓑ fly
   Ⓒ sky
   Ⓓ my

7   Which word does not have the same vowel sound as <u>fence</u>?

   Ⓐ bread
   Ⓑ cent
   Ⓒ feet
   Ⓓ jest

8   Which word has the same beginning sound as <u>thin</u>?

   Ⓐ than
   Ⓑ those
   Ⓒ that
   Ⓓ thick

9   Which word has the same vowel sound as <u>cloud</u>?

   Ⓐ clock
   Ⓑ now
   Ⓒ should
   Ⓓ book

10 Which word has the same vowel sound as <u>weigh</u>?

   Ⓐ receive
   Ⓑ wheel
   Ⓒ ate
   Ⓓ believe

11 Which word does not have the same vowel sound as <u>bird</u>?

Ⓐ skirt

Ⓑ chair

Ⓒ learn

Ⓓ turn

12 Which word is a compound word?

Ⓐ sunflower

Ⓑ window

Ⓒ wonderful

Ⓓ silliness

13 The contraction for <u>they have</u> is:

Ⓐ the've

Ⓑ they've

Ⓒ they'ave

Ⓓ tha've

14 The contraction for <u>will not</u> is:

Ⓐ willn't

Ⓑ will'nt

Ⓒ won'nt

Ⓓ won't

15 <u>Wonderful</u> has how many syllables?

Ⓐ 1

Ⓑ 2

Ⓒ 3

Ⓓ 4

(See page 99 for answer key.)

CHAPTER 3

Vocabulary

If your child is to read and write well, he must have a solid understanding of words. Words aren't just a series of letters strung together whose sounds create a recognizable part of our language; words have *meaning*. A child who is reading a story about a kiwi will have a hard time understanding the story if he doesn't know that a kiwi is a kind of fruit. At the same time, when expressing ideas in writing, the choice of words directly affects the reader's ability to understand what the author is trying to say.

There are several ways your child can show that he understands the meaning of words. A child can show he understands by being able to choose words that are specific to the context (*The mountain had a very high peak*), and through the ability to use a variety of words with the same meaning (*She was very happy to see her old friend. She was very glad to see her old friend.*).

What Your Third Grader Should Be Learning

By third grade, your child is developing a solid understanding of word meanings. He is learning to recognize synonyms and antonyms and to understand the meaning of words in context. This involves understanding what each word means and how it relates to the sentence. In addition, your child should be able to identify which sentences use a word in a similar way.

What Tests May Ask

This chapter presents concepts often used in standardized tests to assess a student's understanding of the meaning of words. Standardized tests generally use several types of questions to assess a student's knowledge of word meanings. One type of question presents words in isolation.

A <u>book</u> is something to:

(A) eat

(B) sing

(C) play

(D) read

In these situations, if the word isn't familiar, there is nothing within the question to help your child figure out what it means.

Another type of question presents a word in a sentence and asks a child to interpret its meaning. This may be done by presenting a sentence and asking for its meaning.

Please <u>return</u> the book to the library. <u>Return</u> means:

(A) take out

(B) spin

(C) take back

(D) buy

Similarly, the test may present a word in a sentence and ask the student to identify another sentence that uses the word the same way.

> I must water the <u>flower</u> each day so it will grow.
>
> In which sentence does the word <u>flower</u> mean the same thing as in the sentence above?
>
> Ⓐ The dogwood will <u>flower</u> in the spring.
>
> Ⓑ I can't wait for the plant to <u>flower</u>.
>
> Ⓒ I found a pretty yellow <u>flower</u> in my yard.
>
> Ⓓ She will sell the plants once they <u>flower</u>.

As you can see, in order for your child to do well on this section of the test, he needs to know what a word means *and* be able to use the word appropriately. The activities in this chapter are designed to help enhance your child's ability to work with words.

Word Meanings

In addition to being able to define words, children in the third grade should be able to generate or recognize a synonym or an antonym for a specified word. **Synonyms** are words that have the same or almost the same meaning. For example, *large* is a synonym for *big*. In contrast, **antonyms** are words that mean the opposite or almost the opposite of each other. *In* is the opposite of *out*; they are antonyms.

Group standardized tests rarely ask for lengthy definitions. When standardized tests are designed, space is always an issue. A test that is quite long is more expensive to publish, takes too much time away from teaching, and is harder for the student because fatigue can affect the results.

What You and Your Child Can Do

One of the most helpful ways to develop vocabulary is to **read, read, read** to your child. Books provide exposure to vocabulary that we may not use during everyday speech. Similarly, books present words in context, so the words are more meaningful to your child. Not only is it often easier to remember something that is more meaningful, but presenting a word in context helps your child make associations, which broadens his understanding.

Ask Questions. As you enjoy books together, make sure your child understands the words you read. Ask your child directly. After reading the sentence, *The professor worked hard to hide his experiment*, ask: "Do you know what *experiment* means?"

Get Your Child to Help. After reading the above sentence, you could say, "I wonder what a *professor* is?" and have your child help explain the meaning to you.

Keep a Journal. Have your child keep a journal of new words learned, with each new word written on a page. Your child can then make an illustration to explain the word.

Practice. You can help your child use skills from the Word Analysis section on prefixes and suffixes to figure out what an unknown word means. Have your child identify the base word, then look at the meaning of the prefix or suffix.

> The <u>thankless</u> man walked away after retrieving his lost poodle from the boy.

In this sentence, the base word is **thank** and the suffix is **less**; therefore, the meaning is "without thanks." Similarly, a word ending in **-ing** is going to be a verb, so your child can determine that it is some kind of action.

Listen. When you read, have your child listen for ways in which the author uses synonyms and antonyms to make the writing more interesting or more clear. Authors often use the word *or* when they are using two different words of similar meaning or are putting several words together, separated by a comma.

> All the dresses I tried on were <u>tight or snug</u>.

> The mountain had a very <u>dangerous, perilous</u> path.

Authors often use words such as *but, however, yet*, or *rather than* to signal that an opposite or a contrast is being used.

> I thought he had written a *long* story, <u>but</u> it was rather *short*.

> She wanted *more* ice cream <u>rather than</u> *less* ice cream.

> She tried to train the turtle to be *fast*; <u>however</u>, it was quite *slow* in the race.

Schedule an Opposite Day. Have an Opposite Day, in which you and your child speak in opposites. *The crackers made me hungry* really means *The crackers made me full.*

Play A-Word-a-Day. Have your family learn a word a day. As you have dinner, present a word and use it in a sentence. Let your child guess its meaning. Ask your child to use it in a sentence, or provide an antonym or synonym. Listen for its use throughout the next day; how many times did your child use it or hear it? Keep a chart to see which word was used the most.

Rephrase. Rephrase what your child says, using synonyms. The more your child hears words in context, the more his or her vocabulary will grow.

CHILD: That was a pretty dress.

PARENT: It was beautiful, wasn't it?

Make Up Riddles. Children typically enjoy a challenge. While driving in the car or snuggling at bedtime, or when your child helps with dinner, create a playful challenge. Make up a riddle for your child to solve. Ask your child to make up a riddle for you:

> I mean the same thing as <u>speak</u>, and I rhyme with <u>walk</u>. (talk)

You have just created a situation in which you are working with two skills at the same time: vocabulary development (synonyms) and word analysis. The riddles can be adapted to fit the skill you are working on.

> I mean the same thing as <u>ship</u> and I begin the same way as <u>banana</u>. (boat)

> I am the opposite of <u>cold</u> and I have the same vowel sound as <u>octopus</u>. (hot)

> You find me at a birthday party and I mean the same thing as <u>present</u>. (gift)

Create a Challenge. Pick a word and see how many synonyms you and your child can generate. Keep a list of the words with the most synonyms. See how many words you and your child can generate antonyms for before you get stumped; keep the list going as long as possible.

Present your child with a sentence. Challenge your child to restate the sentence using as many synonyms as possible. Have your child make up a sentence for you.

> The pretty garments were delivered to the store.

> The <u>beautiful</u> <u>clothes</u> were delivered to the <u>shop</u>.

Do the same thing with antonyms. Present a sentence and have your child restate it with as many antonyms as possible.

My friend is late for his new class.

My <u>enemy</u> is <u>early</u> for his <u>old</u> class.

Adapt a Game. When you play a board game with your child, add an extra step. After rolling the dice, have your child generate a synonym for a specified word. If correct, give him or her a bonus move.

Play Word Finds. Word finds are grids of letters in which words are hidden either across, up and down, or diagonally. Take graph paper ($\frac{1}{2}$-inch by $\frac{1}{2}$-inch squares) and write 10 to 15 words somewhere in the grid. Then fill in the other spaces with random letters. Give your child a list of ten antonyms or synonyms and see if he can find the hidden matching words. See the sample word find at the end of this chapter.

Use Crossword Puzzles. Use graph paper to create a crossword puzzle. Use either antonyms or synonyms for all the clues.

Words in Context

As previously discussed, standardized tests look at your child's ability to use and understand words in context. In order to become a good reader, your child needs to understand what each word means and how it relates to the sentence. For example, in a story about a kite, the reader needs to understand that *briskly*, in the sentence *The wind blew briskly for many days* means "strong and lively." Otherwise, the reader may not understand why the little girl couldn't fly her kite.

Instead of looking at words in isolation, as in the previous section, this section looks at your child's ability to understand words in the context of a sentence.

All but the _____ boats sank in the storm.

In the above sentence, the context narrows the choice of words that fit and still make sense. Given the following choices,

cozy　weak　beautiful　sturdy

the first three do not maintain the implied meaning of the sentence. Plugging **sturdy** into the blank makes the most sense. "**All but the sturdy boats sank in the storm**" leads to the most logical choice: **cozy, weak,** and **beautiful** don't relate directly to being able to survive a storm. The choice "**weak**" would be appropriate if the sentence were expressing surprise or a contrast; weak boats don't typically last through a storm.

Not only must students understand which words do and don't fit into a sentence, given the sentence's meaning, but they must also understand that words may have more than one meaning. The precise meaning must be determined by looking at the context in which the word is used.

There was a large <u>fly</u> sitting on my window sill.

Did you see the eagle <u>fly</u> up to the top of the tree?

As these sentences illustrate, the word *fly* is both a noun (an object) and a verb (an action). To know what the word means, you must look at the sentence and how the word is used.

There are several ways in which your child can demonstrate that he understands the multiple meaning of words. Your child should be able to use a synonym or short phrase to show understanding of the specified word's meaning.

The <u>bug</u> sat on the window.

Bug in this sentence could be replaced with the word *insect*.

The <u>insect</u> sat on the window.

The detective put a <u>bug</u> in the thief's office.

In contrast, *bug* in this sentence means *listening device*.

The detective put a <u>listening device</u> in the thief's office.

In addition, your child should be able to identify which of several sentences use a word in a similar way. Although specific knowledge of a synonym is not needed, understanding the context of the sentence is still necessary for understanding the word's particular meaning.

We had a <u>fine</u> time at the zoo with our friends.

In which sentence does the word <u>fine</u> mean the same as in the sentence above?

(A) I had to pay a <u>fine</u> at the library.

(B) Her costume was <u>fine</u> for Halloween.

(C) He received a <u>fine</u> for speeding.

In this example, sentence B uses the word *fine* in the same way as the provided sentence. In contrast, sentences A and C use the word *fine* to mean *"a fee."*

What You and Your Child Can Do

Read, Read, Read. Again, reading to your child and having him read on a regular basis increases vocabulary skills. As you read, have your child use the context of the sentence to try to figure out unknown words.

Reading will also increase your child's familiarity with words that have more than one meaning (multi-meaning words). As you read to your child, have him listen for any words that also have a second meaning. Similarly, you should highlight any multi-meaning words. Keep a running list of the words you encounter.

Use Sentence Practice. Give your child a sentence with a word missing. See how many words he can think of that make sense. Discuss which ones are most logical.

The little _____ flew around the backyard. (Leave out the noun or object.)

My book was so _____ that it almost broke my arm. (Leave out the adjective.)

When you _____, make sure you look where you are going. (Leave out the verb.)

Be a Detective. Have your child look through magazines and cut out pictures of things whose words have two or more meanings. These pictures can then be made into a scrapbook. Have your child decorate the cover of the scrapbook and give it a special title.

A second way to be a detective is to have your child look around the house and try to find objects that have a second meaning. For example, a *scale* in the bathroom can be something to measure weight, but a *scale* is also found in music and *scales* cover the body of a fish. Similarly, the *batter* used in a cake mix is very different from the *batter* in a baseball game. These multi-meaning words can be drawn, one word per page, and made into a special scrapbook or journal. As an alternative, your child could make a list of these words and see how long the list can grow.

Have your child plug each choice into the sentence in the specified spot, then reread the sentence or phrase and check to make sure it makes sense. Make sure your child reads all the choices, even if he thinks he knows the right one.

An example of how to plug in each choice follows:

Directions: Which of the following words fits both sentences?

    Please _____ all of the same books together.

    We had a very large _____ of people at our party.

- Ⓐ put
- Ⓑ find
- Ⓒ group
- Ⓓ remember

Your child should repeat each of the following sentences silently in his head to determine which choice is accurate.

- Ⓐ Please <u>put</u> all of the same books together.

    We had a very large <u>put</u> of people at our party.
- Ⓑ Please <u>find</u> all of the same books together.

    We had a very large <u>find</u> of people at our party.
- Ⓒ Please <u>group</u> all of the same books together.

    We had a very large <u>group</u> of people at our party.
- Ⓓ Please <u>remember</u> all of the same books together.

    We had a very large <u>remember</u> of people at our party.

TIP

As you work with these activities, if you are having difficulty coming up with words or sentences, open a book and use examples from any page.

Practice Skill: Vocabulary

Directions: In the following examples, choose the word that means the same as the underlined word.

1 A <u>library</u> is a place to:
- Ⓐ sing
- Ⓑ read
- Ⓒ swim
- Ⓓ play

---

2 A <u>beetle</u> is a kind of:
- Ⓐ stone
- Ⓑ bread
- Ⓒ song
- Ⓓ insect

---

3 To <u>depart</u> is to:
- Ⓐ arrive
- Ⓑ break
- Ⓒ leave
- Ⓓ learn

---

4 To <u>repair</u> is to:
- Ⓐ fix
- Ⓑ take apart
- Ⓒ cut in half
- Ⓓ eat

Directions: Read the example sentence, and then choose a sentence that uses the underlined word in the same way.

5 I need to <u>hand</u> in my report today.
- Ⓐ My <u>hand</u> is very cold.
- Ⓑ I need to <u>hand</u> the menu to the waiter.
- Ⓒ Put your <u>hand</u> on the top of the ball.

6 We took a short <u>break</u> during math class.

   Ⓐ My favorite glass did not <u>break</u> when it fell.

   Ⓑ Her hand will <u>break</u> the egg if she is not careful.

   Ⓒ We got a drink of water during the <u>break</u>.

7 I have three <u>brushes</u> for my hair.

   Ⓐ He <u>brushes</u> the horses every day.

   Ⓑ The cat knocked her <u>brushes</u> to the floor.

   Ⓒ She <u>brushes</u> the hair from her coat.

8 My <u>dresses</u> were back from the cleaners.

   Ⓐ The store put its best <u>dresses</u> in the window.

   Ⓑ She must stand as she <u>dresses</u> the models.

   Ⓒ She <u>dresses</u> herself very well.

Directions: Read the sentence. Choose the answer that means the same as the underlined word.

9 Betty used a key to <u>unlock</u> her car. Unlock means:

   Ⓐ wash
   Ⓑ open
   Ⓒ drive
   Ⓓ park

10 Robert was <u>pleased</u> with his drawing.

   Ⓐ annoyed
   Ⓑ upset
   Ⓒ satisfied
   Ⓓ worried

11 We will <u>likely</u> have rain tomorrow.

   Ⓐ never
   Ⓑ seldom
   Ⓒ quickly
   Ⓓ probably

12 John <u>often</u> goes to the mountains.

   Ⓐ frequently
   Ⓑ rarely
   Ⓒ sadly
   Ⓓ never

Directions: Use the words in the sentence to help you figure out what the underlined words mean.

13 We had <u>few</u> books so we needed to share with each other. <u>Few</u> means:

   Ⓐ many
   Ⓑ torn
   Ⓒ limited
   Ⓓ no

14 The ants will <u>gather</u> seeds from the plants. <u>Gather</u> means:

   Ⓐ spill
   Ⓑ collect
   Ⓒ destroy
   Ⓓ eat

15 The skater <u>twirled</u> around the rink without falling. <u>Twirled</u> means:

- Ⓐ looked
- Ⓑ marched
- Ⓒ spun
- Ⓓ sang

Directions: Choose the word that best fits the sentence.

16 The little girl was afraid of the _____ lion.

- Ⓐ roaring
- Ⓑ small
- Ⓒ sleeping
- Ⓓ golden

17 The runners were _____ at the finish line.

- Ⓐ surprised
- Ⓑ tired
- Ⓒ worried
- Ⓓ whispering

18 The _____ made the sky as dark as night.

- Ⓐ airplanes
- Ⓑ storm
- Ⓒ sun
- Ⓓ moon

(See page 99 for answer key.)

Word Find

Directions: Find and circle the opposites of the words listed below in the word find graph. They can be across, up and down, or diagonal.

in *out*   late *early*   up *down*   true *False*   leave   old *New*

walk *Run*   pretty *ugly*   slow *Fast*   smile   happy *Sad*   clean *dirty*

long *Short*   wild *calm*   best   (See page 99 for answer key.)

```
S   H   E   L   W   B   T   A
N   E   W   V   D   O   W   N
F   O   U   N   T   N   Y   F
Y   F   T   U   R   A   R   C
S   T   U   R   O   R   M   A
O   I   R   S   H   E   G   A
T   U   M   I   S   E   R   R
T   R   L   W   D   Y   W   S
S   O   U   T   L   N   I   N
A   F   U   G   H   E   F   A
F   G   U   H   R   S   A   D
O   N   B   M   E   Z   L   D
L   W   H   S   N   J   S   E
W   O   R   S   T   X   E   O
T   R   F   R   E   T   E   R
F   F   E   A   R   L   Y   X
G   C   K   H   E   N   A   J
```

CHAPTER 4

Reading Comprehension

In Chapter 3, we looked at the need to understand the meaning of individual words while also learning that the overall sentence can be a very important part of understanding the meaning of a particular word. Now we will discuss reading comprehension, which involves how well a child can understand what a piece of writing is about.

What Your Third Grader Should Be Learning

Your child should be reading a variety of books and be able to remember the details of what she has read, including the sequence of events and the facts from the story. In addition, your third-grade child should be learning study skills, including how to use reference books such as encyclopedias, dictionaries, and atlases.

What Tests May Ask

The reading comprehension section of standardized tests assesses the child's recall of information as it is presented within a story. In addition, this section looks at the child's ability to associate individual pieces of information and to understand how they fit together to form a story. Several different kinds of questions are typically asked of third graders in their reading curriculum.

To be a good reader, you must have good literal recall, which means that you must be able to remember the details of what you read. Details can include everything from the sequence of events, a fact from the story (Mary was sad), and cause and effect when told directly.

Reading comprehension also measures more advanced thinking skills that require the reader to go beyond the basic facts that are obvious from the story. For example, your child will be asked to determine the main idea of a story or to make an inference based on what happened in the story. The answers to these kinds of questions are not told explicitly by the author.

Consider the following short story:

It was Tuesday, and Mary was very happy because the sun was shining. She had been hoping that the rain would stop because she wanted to ride her new bike that she'd gotten for her birthday last Sunday. Three whole days, and she hadn't been able to ride her bike yet! The bike was much bigger than her old one, and it was blue—her favorite color. After Mary got dressed, she ran downstairs to eat her breakfast. After pulling on her coat, she called "Goodbye" to her mother and ran outside. Mary put on her helmet, got her bike from the shed, and then took off down the driveway. Although she wobbled at first, she soon got the knack of riding the bigger bike and was able to coast in and out of the trees in her backyard without falling.

Here are examples of typical questions assessing literal comprehension that your child might encounter on a standardized test.

1. *Sequence of events*: What happened before Mary ate her breakfast? (She got dressed.)

   What did Mary do after she got her bike from the shed? (Rode down the driveway.)

2. *Fact from the story:* How was the bike different from her old bike? (It was bigger.)

   What color was the bike? (It was blue.)

3. *Cause and effect:* Why did Mary get a new bike? (It was a birthday present.)

   What made Mary happy? (The sun was shining.)

4. *Main idea:* Stories are always written *about* something, about some topic the author wants to share. When you read, you find out what the writer is interested in telling you. To find the main idea, you must determine what the story is about, what its topic is, and what special or unique points the author is trying to make about the topic.

In the story above, the main idea is that **Mary got a new bike for her birthday**. *Mary's new bike is blue* or *Mary prepares to ride her bike* are both true about the story, but they are just details; they don't cover the main or most important information in the story.

Inferential Comprehension

When we read, we get information directly from the author: *The blue dress was pretty*. We know from this sentence that the dress was blue and we know the person saying this thought it was pretty. However, if the author told us everything she wanted us to know in a direct manner, the story would probably not be very interesting. Therefore, authors count on us to make inferences (to read between the lines) when they write a story.

In order to get information inferentially from a story, you must be able to detect clues.

However, you must also be very careful not to read too much into some sentences, or you will misinterpret what the author means. For example, consider the following sentence:

The line outside the ice cream store stretched to the end of the block.

An inference from this could be that many people go to this ice cream store because the ice cream is very good. However, this is not the only conclusion that can be drawn. Perhaps:

• The store is shorthanded on that particular day so service is quite slow.

• It's the only ice cream store in town and the movie next door just let out.

• The store only has a take-out window and the store is at the end of the block.

The three alternative conclusions say nothing about the quality of the ice cream. In this instance, we need more information to determine an appropriate inference.

Questions that tap inferential thinking take information in the story and put it together so that new information can be gained. The process involves drawing conclusions from what is read. In the story about Mary and her new bike, we can draw many inferences:

The weather was rainy from Sunday, the day of her birthday, until Tuesday. (She hadn't been able to ride her bike yet.)

She had grown. (The new bike was bigger than her old one.)

It was cool outside. (She put a coat on.)

She did not live in the city. (She had many trees in her backyard.)

Critical Reading

Critical reading involves evaluating what is read. Readers need to determine whether the information is a **fact** or an **opinion**. A fact is something that all readers would determine from the sentence; it exists or occurs. An opinion, on the other hand, is someone's belief based on her personal ideas: *The blue dress was pretty.* It is a **fact** that the dress was blue. Anyone looking at it who was not color-blind would draw the same conclusion. However, it is an **opinion** that the dress was pretty. It may be pretty to me, but you may not particularly like it; therefore it is not pretty to you.

Critical reading further evaluates whether the information is fantasy or reality. Fantasy is a kind of story that isn't real, that's not possible in our world. Animals that talk, cars that fly, and beanstalks that grow to the sky are all examples of fantasy. Reality, on the other hand, could possibly happen.

What You and Your Child Can Do

By now, you've probably realized that reading is an excellent tool for enhancing your child's education. There are several ways you can encourage your child's interest in reading.

Set an Example. Provide a reading time at least once a week for 30 minutes in which the whole family reads together in one room. The TV is off, nobody answers the phone or doorbell, and conversation is off limits. Show your child how to stick with a book; if you show good concentration, your child is more likely to do so. Take some time at the end of the half hour to discuss interesting parts of the book. Use this as a sharing time.

Let Your Child Choose the Book. Children won't necessarily like the books we did when we were their age. If the book seems like an easy one for your child, that's okay; she's still reading. If child wants to read a magazine, that's okay too.

Have a Daily Reading Requirement. Reading for 20 to 30 minutes before bedtime can be an excellent way to wind down from the day and make bedtime less stressful.

Ask Questions. When you read to your child, use the time to enhance her comprehension skills. Ask questions as you read. Be careful: If your child perceives this reading time as a drill session, she may not want to be read to any more. That would be too bad, because reading is such an important skill for success in the classroom.

Put your child in the expert role. Ask questions as if you didn't remember, or aren't sure about the conclusion. Make the time more of a discussion than a class. Giving your child lots of genuine praise for careful reading and good thinking during your discussions will enhance continued effort.

Try these questions:

Who ...	*Who did such and such?*
What ...	*What do you think made so and so do that?*
Why ...	*Why are they going there?*
When ...	*When did she?*
Where ...	*Where was?*
How ...	*How did they?*
Which ...	*Which one was?*

- Talk about feelings: How do you think so and so felt when ... Why was Mary feeling ... ?

- Discuss the purpose of or motive for certain actions: Why did so and so do that?

- Discuss cause and effect: What made such and such happen?

- Make predictions: What do you think will happen next? How do you know?

- Come up with another title for the story or chapter, using the main idea.

- Discuss characteristics of a character: What kind of a friend would so and so make? Why? Why were so and so friends but not this other person?

- Remember that tests often assess a skill in a somewhat indirect way. Give your child practice with this by posing questions that ask for a negative: What is something that could *not* happen next? Which of these titles is *not* the best?

Types of Reading

In addition to stories, children are exposed to flyers, birthday invitations, and instructions for projects. These require different reading skills than a story, because the information is organized in a different manner, presented more concisely and often includes numbers.

As the opportunity arises, give your child plenty of experience reading different types of information. Ask questions and have your child show you where on the flyer, party invitation, and so on a piece of information came from.

Study Skills

In elementary school, students spend many years learning to read so that in middle school they can use their reading skills to learn. In addition, the elementary school years introduce students to basic study skills. These include learning where to find various kinds of information and how to use basic resources.

Students in third grade learn that books can be either *fiction* or *nonfiction*. A book that is nonfiction relates facts and information that is true or real. A book that is fiction is not true: The content is made up, not based on fact. Nonfiction books include encyclopedias (which provide information in many areas of learning) and dictionaries (which give the meaning and pronunciation of words). Students in third grade also learn that an atlas contains maps. Many begin to use the newspaper to learn about current events.

In order to use these sources of information, several skills are necessary. Alphabetizing words, using the guide words on a page, and reading a dictionary entry are all skills that may be presented on standardized tests.

Alphabetizing

Your third grader should be learning how to alphabetize to the third letter. Words are alphabetized by their first letter.

<u>a</u>pple

<u>d</u>inner

<u>s</u>ister

If all of the first letters are the same, then you must look at the second letters.

<u>ma</u>mmal

<u>mo</u>untain

<u>mu</u>stard

If all of the second letters are the same, then you must look at the *third* letter.

<u>sha</u>rp

<u>she</u>ep

<u>shr</u>imp

Dictionary Skills

Guide Words

In addition to working with alphabetical order, efficient use of a dictionary requires being able to use *guide words*. These are the words at the top of the page that tell you the first word on the page and the last word on the page. If a word, using alphabetical order, falls in between these two guide words, it will be found on that page.

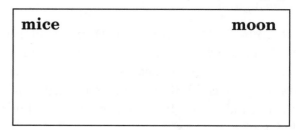

mice	**moon**

Look at the sample dictionary page with guide words *mice* and *moon* at the top. On that page, you would find *mitten* but not *man,* because when alphabetizing, *man* comes before *mice*, the first word on the page. On the same page, you would find *moo* but not *mud,* because mud comes after *moon*, the last word on the page.

Dictionary Entries

In addition to guide words, your child should be familiar with dictionary entries. A dictionary entry includes the correct spelling of the word together with information about how to pronounce it, how it is broken into syllables, and what its various meanings are:

> **oboe** \ō′-bō\ a woodwind instrument shaped like a tube with holes, keys, and a reed mouthpiece.

From this dictionary entry, we know that an oboe is a musical instrument with two syllables (*o* and *bo*) and that the two *o*'s have the long vowel sound.

What You and Your Child Can Do

Problem Solve. When the opportunity arises, ask your child where you should look to answer a question. For example, if you are talking about lions, ask your child where you could find out what they eat (an encyclopedia). When reading, if you come across a word your child doesn't know, ask where to find out (the dictionary), then look the word up with your child.

Practice

1. Name a word and have your child look it up in the dictionary. You can make a game out of it by timing your child and keeping track of which word was found the fastest and which word took the longest time. See if your child can beat her own record.

2. Give your child two words and have her determine a word that would go in between when alphabetizing.

present	_____	print
wagon	_____	whale
raccoon	_____	rake

3. Open to a page on the dictionary. Cover all but the two guide words. See if your child can name a word that is on the page. Check to see if it is there.

4. Give your child lists of words to alphabetize. Note which type of list gives your child the most difficulty and make up more as needed.

List A	*List B*	*List C*
camel	cat	dinner
violin	crayon	ditch
sea	clown	dime
bat	circle	dish

List A looks at first letter only: bat camel sea violin.

List B looks at the first and second letters: cat circle clown crayon.

List C looks at the first, second, and third letters: dime dinner dish ditch.

Practice Skill: Reading Comprehension

Directions: Read the following questions and choose the correct answer from the four choices.

1 Which word would you find on the following dictionary page, with guide words "robin" and "role"?

robin	role

Ⓐ round   Ⓑ robot
Ⓒ rope   Ⓓ rule

2 Which word would you find on the dictionary page below, with guide words "motor" and "move"?

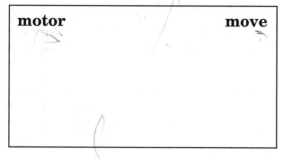

motor   **move**

  Ⓐ much
  Ⓑ month
  Ⓒ motto
  Ⓓ music

3 Which word would you NOT find on the dictionary page below, with guide words "pride" and "proper"?

pride   **proper**

  Ⓐ princess
  Ⓑ practice
  Ⓒ progress
  Ⓓ program

4 If you wanted to find out what food an elephant eats, where would you look?

  Ⓐ dictionary
  Ⓑ atlas
  Ⓒ encyclopedia
  Ⓓ newspaper

Directions: Read the following short story. What sentence would most likely come next?

Yesterday I went for a walk in the woods. When I got tired, I sat down next to a tree. A beautiful yellow butterfly came to rest on a small rock. I walked slowly over to it, holding my net in front of me.

5 Ⓐ A squirrel climbed down the tree beside me.

    Ⓑ I let the net fall and then held the butterfly carefully.

    Ⓒ The sun shone brightly over my head.

    Ⓓ The birds were chirping loudly in the trees.

Directions: Read the following short story. What sentence would most likely come next?

A large dragon lived in a dark cave. Nobody knew the dragon was there. One day, some children were playing in front of the cave. They heard loud noises coming from inside. They decided to see what was making the noise.

6 Ⓐ They ran to the water to cool off their feet.

    Ⓑ The children sat on their blankets to eat their lunch.

    Ⓒ Slowly and quietly, they entered the cave with their flashlights.

    Ⓓ They played hide and seek around the cave until it got dark.

Directions: Read the following story. Then answer the questions.

All Saturday morning, Sally waited for her friend Jane to come over. While she waited, she worked on an art project. They'd been planning to go to the park since there was no school today. When they talked last night, they decided that they would take a picnic lunch, a blanket to sit on, and Jane's dog, Fuzzy. After eating their favorite lunch of peanut butter and jelly sandwiches, they would throw the Frisbee around and try to teach Fuzzy to catch it. If the weather was warm enough, they would even try to get Fuzzy to go for a swim in the pond.

Sally noticed that her stomach was starting to growl. When she looked at her watch, she saw that it was 12:30 p.m. She had been working on her project for three hours! Jane was late. Sally wasn't sure what she should do.

Just then, the doorbell rang. Sally was very happy to see her friend Jane at the door.

7 Why did the girls decide to go to the park?

Ⓐ It was sunny.
Ⓑ They had finished their homework.
Ⓒ There was no school.
Ⓓ They wanted to meet their friend.

8 When did Sally start to work on her art project?

Ⓐ 8:30
Ⓑ 9:30
Ⓒ 9:00
Ⓓ 10:30

9 How do you think Sally felt when Jane arrived?

Ⓐ sad
Ⓑ angry
Ⓒ worried
Ⓓ happy

10 What did Sally do after she finished her art project?

Ⓐ Made lunch.
Ⓑ Gathered the Frisbee, blanket, and sandwiches.
Ⓒ Looked at her watch.
Ⓓ Called Jane.

11 Which of the following is the best title for this story?

Ⓐ The Picnic
Ⓑ A Day Off from School
Ⓒ Throwing Frisbees
Ⓓ The Late Friend

12 What made Sally look at her watch?

Ⓐ She finished her art project.
Ⓑ Her stomach was growling.
Ⓒ Jane arrived at her house.
Ⓓ She forgot to make sandwiches.

13 In the sentence, **She noticed that it was 12:30,** underline{noticed} means:

Ⓐ was told
Ⓑ became aware
Ⓒ forgot
Ⓓ remembered

(See page 99 for answer key.)

CHAPTER 5

Language Mechanics

When children write, they not only use words to express their thoughts and ideas, but they also use aspects of language mechanics to help them convey information to the reader. Language mechanics include both the seemingly little things that make the written word easier to understand (punctuation marks and capitalization) and grammar (word usage, sentence structure).

What Your Third Grader Should Be Learning

By third grade, your child is more likely to write in complete sentences and his written stories will include more detail. In addition, third grade is the time to learn and use more varied punctuation marks and to expand on the use of capital letters, with the expectation that consistency in use becomes the norm.

What Tests May Ask

This chapter outlines language mechanics skills that your child may encounter on standardized tests. In addition, attention is paid to how standardized tests assess these skills, as this format is typically very different from how they are assessed within the classroom.

Capitalization

The third-grade curriculum focuses on the use of capital letters in a variety of situations. These include:

- the first letter of all sentences,
- all proper names,
- initials within a name,
- the beginning of a sentence within a quote, and
- the salutation in a letter.

Punctuation

By third grade, students should be able to punctuate the end of a sentence using *periods, question marks,* and *exclamation points* appropriately.

We saw a tall tree at the park.

Did you see the elephant at the zoo?

Wow! That dog barks very loud!

Your child should also be familiar with *quotation marks* used to show that someone is talking or to show exactly what was said by someone. (Bill said, "That was an exciting movie.")

Commas are used in several situations, including:

- To set off items in a list—I need carrots, bread, and milk.
- To set off a direct quote—"Let's go for a swim," Debbie said.
- To separate a dependent clause—After the movie, the boys left.
- In dates—October 12, 2000.

Apostrophes can be troublesome for third graders. They are used within a contraction (don't) and to show possession (Susie's ball).

Underlining is used for titles of books.

Sentence Structure

By third grade, children are expected to know how to express a meaningful idea or complete thought by writing in complete sentences. Your child should understand that sentences have a subject (the *who* or *what* of the sentence) and a predicate (the words that tell what the subject does or is).

> The boys played baseball in the backyard.

In the above sentence, the subject is *boys*; that's who the sentence is about. The complete predicate is *played baseball in the backyard* (that's what the boys did). The following group of words is not a complete sentence (it's not a complete, meaningful thought) and therefore it's disqualified as a sentence:

> My house and tall trees.

This may be somewhat confusing to your child because it begins with a capital letter and ends with a period; but punctuation does not make a sentence!!

Sentence structure also taps the grammatical structure of the sentence. Not only must you have a subject and a predicate, but there must be agreement between the different parts of the sentence. The subject must agree with the verb form. The verb tense must agree with the sentence's time frame. Consider the following sentence:

> We are listen to music while we watched the game.

In this sentence, the verb form **listen** is inaccurate; it should be **We are *listening***. In addition, the first part of the sentence is happening now: **We *are* listening**. In contrast, **we *watched* the game** is an action that already happened. You can't be doing something now and a while ago at the same time. The parts of this sentence are not in agreement.

Word Usage: Pronouns

Third graders also learn about pronouns, those small words that stand for nouns. Remember, nouns are people, places, or things. *He, she, it, we, me, us,* and *they* are all pronouns, referring to the person, place, or thing.

Your child is already using pronouns within his everyday language, so this is likely something he already knows. But because information presented in a different context can be confusing, helping your child to recognize what pronouns are may prove beneficial.

> <u>The book</u> is on the shelf. <u>It</u> is on the shelf.
>
> <u>Susie</u> had a birthday party. <u>She</u> had a birthday party.
>
> <u>Matthew</u> hit a home run. <u>He</u> hit a home run.
>
> <u>Robbie, Katie, and Sam</u> are going to the zoo. <u>They</u> are going to the zoo.
>
> <u>Ryan and I</u> would like to have lunch now, please. <u>We</u> would like to have lunch now, please.

Spelling

Because of its multiple-choice format, a standardized test looks at a child's ability to identify the correct spelling of a word rather than his ability to come up with the spelling on his own. Instead of a typical spelling test like those given during regular classwork, standardized tests of spelling are really more like proofreading: being able to recognize when a word is spelled incorrectly. When completing this type of question, remind your child not to look at the words for too long. Overthinking can cause students to change an answer to an incorrect one.

To determine your child's overall spelling skill, look at his weekly spelling tests. Is your child learning the words presented each week?

Is your child then spelling these words correctly in everyday writing? To enhance your child's spelling skills, use the words being presented within the classroom; keep a list of words misspelled on the spelling tests and look for frequently misspelled words in daily writing.

What You and Your Child Can Do

One way to enhance spelling accuracy is to use a multisensory approach with problem words. Have your child trace the word while saying each sound aloud, then cover the word and write it three times from memory. This process should be repeated until your child achieves success. To make this fun, you can have your child trace the word in shaving cream or pudding while saying the sounds aloud! In addition, when your child is correcting spelling errors, work on having your child identify the rule being used. This creates an association between reading and writing, thereby making spelling a more meaningful task.

Homonyms (words that sound alike but have different meanings and are spelled differently, such as know and no) are frequently misspelled. As you check your child's work, look for this type of error.

Practice, Practice, Practice. As previously noted, this section of standardized tests will likely be least familiar to your child. Consequently, it may be helpful for your child to practice identifying errors. The practice test at the end of the chapter will give you the opportunity to see how your child approaches this format: Is your child having a particularly difficult time following the format? Does he find the errors without much effort? Can he recognize the errors when looking carefully?

If your child is having a problem, you need to determine whether it is due to the format or to your child's less developed skill in language mechanics. One way to determine this is to go over your child's answers with him. Ask your child to tell you why a particular response was chosen; is your child verbalizing relevant but inaccurate reasoning?

> **TIP**
>
> **Make sure your child reads all choices before deciding which to choose.**

EXAMPLE:

My <u>friend</u> is <u>jumpping</u> down from a <u>tall</u>
  Ⓐ   Ⓑ   Ⓒ

<u>tree.</u>
Ⓓ

Suppose your child identified response "C" (tall). If your child stated that this was the error because this word should be spelled *talle*, then you would know that your child understood the format (find the error) but did not have solid command of spelling. Your focus then would be on helping to enhance your child's spelling abilities.

EXAMPLE:

My <u>friend</u> is <u>jumpping</u> down from a <u>tall</u>
  Ⓐ   Ⓑ   Ⓒ

<u>tree.</u>
Ⓓ

In this example, suppose your child had chosen "D," stating that this should be an exclamation point. Although that's not necessarily an inaccurate option for this sentence based on the sentence's meaning, it would be incorrect in this example. The reason is that each question will have ***only one*** error. Again, this highlights the need for your child to read all choices before choosing the one he thinks is accurate; your child must choose the *best* response, given the options.

Give your child a couple of practice items each day. Repeat skills that he may be having some difficulty with. Thus, if your child's spelling isn't strong, make up questions that test spelling skills. Use the Word Analysis section for content areas; these are the skills your child has been exposed to in the classroom. If punctuation is weak, make up items to work on this area.

After your child has developed some proficiency, make sure your practice items cover more than one content area. It will be important that your child be able to switch the focus of his thinking from one item to the next (that is, question one is spelling, question two is punctuation, question three is spelling, question four is sentence structure, question five is sentence structure). If you have trouble coming up with practice items, pick one of your child's books and take sentences from it. Modify a word or two to put in the appropriate error.

Have a Pronoun Day. Pick a day and state that every time a pronoun is used, the speaker must say what it stands for. Or, every time a word is used that has a pronoun, rephrase the sentence with the pronoun.

> Dad, I'll take it for you—the tool.
>
> Mom, I'm going to Susie's house.
> Mom, I'm going to her house.

Put a chip or penny in a bowl for each time this is done. Allow your child to trade these in for an extra story before bed or a family game after dinner.

Play Buzz. Decide on a day when your child is to listen for incomplete sentences. Explain that an incomplete sentence is not a complete thought. Whenever your child hears you say an incomplete sentence, he should say *Buzz*. Keep track of all the times your child catches you.

Give Constructive Feedback. When your child makes a grammatical error, it is important that you provide feedback so your child hears the proper way to say the sentence. However, too much criticism can damage his self-esteem and cause him to stop listening to you altogether. The way you offer feedback to your children is very important. Your response should incorporate what your child said, but in its correct form.

CHILD: *Mom, I don't want no more cookies.*

YOU: ***You don't want <u>any</u> more cookies, George?***

CHILD: *No thanks, Mom.*

In the preceding example, Mom corrected George's double negative (*don't ... no*) by rephrasing what he said in question form.

As your child completes written assignments at home, ask him to look for any mistakes before you offer corrections. Even if your child is unable to give you the correct spelling for a particular word, being able to identify it as an error is an important skill.

Practice Skill: Capitalization and Punctuation

Directions: Choose the letter beneath the error in each sentence.

1 <u>Don't</u> you <u>know</u> who I <u>am.</u>
   Ⓐ   Ⓑ   Ⓒ   Ⓓ

2 When <u>mr.</u> Smith arrived, the sailor
   Ⓐ Ⓑ

   asked, <u>"Where</u> have you been<u>?"</u>
              Ⓒ   Ⓓ

3 <u>the</u> <u>farmers</u> looked <u>wet,</u> tired, and
   Ⓐ   Ⓑ   Ⓒ   Ⓓ

   hungry.

4 <u>It</u> <u>wasnt</u> the <u>monkey</u> who ate the <u>pie!</u>
   Ⓐ Ⓑ   Ⓒ   Ⓓ

5 <u>The</u> <u>soldier's</u> marched right up to
   Ⓐ   Ⓑ

   <u>them,</u> as they stood on the <u>wall.</u>
    Ⓒ   Ⓓ

6 <u>I</u> would like you to buy <u>pretzels</u>
   Ⓐ   Ⓑ

   <u>apples,</u> and <u>cheese.</u>
    Ⓒ   Ⓓ

7 It's 4 oclock and we have to go home.
   Ⓐ   Ⓑ   Ⓒ   Ⓓ

8 we heard the crows making a lot of
  Ⓐ   Ⓑ   Ⓒ

noise.
  Ⓓ

9 "I'm afraid that I won't finish my
  Ⓐ

work today, said Mr. Smith.
    Ⓑ   Ⓒ   Ⓓ

10 My birthday is on October 23, 1994
  Ⓐ   Ⓑ   Ⓒ Ⓓ

11 I took off my mitten's, hat, and scarf.
  Ⓐ   Ⓑ   Ⓒ   Ⓓ

(See page 99 for answer key.)

Practice Skill: Sentence Structure

Directions: For each of the following questions, choose "yes" if it is a sentence and "no" if it is not a sentence.

12 The people were singing in very loud.

  Ⓐ yes
  Ⓑ no

13 The sailors looked wet on their boat.

  Ⓐ yes
  Ⓑ no

14 The monkey jumped out of the tree.

  Ⓐ yes
  Ⓑ no

15 The soccer team beat every.

  Ⓐ yes
  Ⓑ no

16 All of the guests in the dog house.

  Ⓐ yes
  Ⓑ no

17 I would like you.

  Ⓐ yes
  Ⓑ no

18 He lived in the house with his aunt.

  Ⓐ yes
  Ⓑ no

19 The people in the park.

  Ⓐ yes
  Ⓑ no

20 I stopped right away and listened.

  Ⓐ yes
  Ⓑ no

(See page 99 for answer key.)

Practice Skill: Word Usage

Directions: Find the error in word usage in each sentence.

21 Jane has many animals on his farm.
    Ⓐ   Ⓑ   Ⓒ   Ⓓ

22 <u>How</u> many <u>toes</u> <u>does</u> a walrus <u>has</u>?

Ⓐ   Ⓑ Ⓒ   Ⓓ

23 His <u>friend</u> <u>were</u> all <u>graceful</u> <u>divers</u>.

Ⓐ   Ⓑ   Ⓒ   Ⓓ

24 The <u>bird</u> <u>flied</u> into the forest

    Ⓐ   Ⓑ

<u>searching</u> for <u>food</u>.

  Ⓒ   Ⓓ

25 The <u>bikes</u> <u>were</u> very loud when <u>it</u>

    Ⓐ Ⓑ   Ⓒ

fell <u>over</u>.

  Ⓓ

26 The boy <u>watch</u> the rabbit <u>run</u> <u>quickly</u>

     Ⓐ   Ⓑ Ⓒ

to the <u>bush</u>.

   Ⓓ

27 We <u>catched</u> the <u>crows</u> <u>eating</u> the <u>food</u>.

   Ⓐ   Ⓑ Ⓒ   Ⓓ

28 <u>I'm</u> afraid that I <u>willn't</u> finish my

 Ⓐ   Ⓑ

<u>homework</u> in <u>time</u>.

  Ⓒ   Ⓓ

Directions: Find the misspelled word in each sentence.

29 I <u>brought</u> my <u>paintings</u> <u>too</u> the <u>fair</u>.

   Ⓐ   Ⓑ   Ⓒ   Ⓓ

30 The <u>pond</u> was <u>behind</u> <u>there</u> <u>house</u>.

   Ⓐ   Ⓑ   Ⓒ   Ⓓ

31 The <u>frogs</u> were <u>hoping</u> <u>across</u> the

   Ⓐ   Ⓑ   Ⓒ

<u>lawn</u>.

 Ⓓ

32 We <u>road</u> to the <u>big</u> <u>game</u> on a <u>bumpy</u>

   Ⓐ   Ⓑ Ⓒ   Ⓓ

bus.

Directions: Choose the word that best completes the sentence.

33 Joan is _____ her picture to her mother.

  Ⓐ shown
  Ⓑ showing
  Ⓒ shows

34 She will _____ her teeth tonight.

  Ⓐ brush
  Ⓑ brushes
  Ⓒ brushing

35 Kay _____ that she did the work correctly.

- Ⓐ known
- Ⓑ knowing
- Ⓒ knows

36 The birds had _____ south for the winter.

- Ⓐ flew
- Ⓑ flying
- Ⓒ flown

37 When the phone rang, Bill _____ it.

- Ⓐ answers
- Ⓑ answered
- Ⓒ answering

(See page 99 for answer key.)

After your child completes each sample test, go over the answers and review mistakes. Then have your child take a red pencil and correct the mistake on the test. It can be very helpful for some children to see the correction within the actual sentence; the different color highlights the correction. On the incomplete sentences section, have your child finish the sentence with an appropriate ending. For example: ***Don't you?*** could be finished, ***Don't you like ice cream?***

CHAPTER 6

Math Concepts

Basic concepts in math are the building blocks on which more advanced mathematical procedures are built. For example, in order to add multi-digit numbers, one needs to have a solid understanding of place value. Being able to work easily with these building blocks makes learning math a less daunting task. Before discussing the concepts, however, it's important to review some terminology.

A *digit* is any of the symbols 0 through 9. These are used to represent a *number*, which is a unit within the mathematical system. *Numeration* refers to the system of numbers that we use. Numbers become a system because they follow a prescribed, universal sequence and hold certain properties true. A number is really a symbol that has a certain value.

What Your Third Grader Should Be Learning

Math concepts in the third-grade curriculum include an understanding of numbers as a sequence that follows a prescribed order in which the difference between any two consecutive numbers is always the same. Place value designates a digit's value based on its position within a number. In addition, during this year your child will continue to expand her ability to compare numbers and to recognize numerical properties.

Sequence

By third grade, students not only count in sequence, but they are also able to skip count. This means they can state every set number, with those numbers in between omitted. For example, skip counting by tens is: 10, 20, 30, 40, 50, 60, 70, 80, 90, 100. Your child should be able to skip count by twos, fives, and tens without much difficulty. In third grade, students also skip count by other numbers, such as threes or fours, as a precursor to multiplication.

Place Value

Place value is a second important concept in mathematics. It refers to the value of the digit, relative to its location in the number. The place value can be identified for any given digit in a written number; in the number 7403, the digit 4 is in the hundreds place and stands for 400. The 3 in 34 is not the same as the 3 in 23, even though both digits are 3. This is because the 3 in 34 is in the tens place and therefore worth 30, while the 3 in 23 is in the ones place and worth only 3. Your child is developing an understanding of place value up to at least the thousands. (This also means that she needs to practice skip counting starting with any number up to one thousand: 326, 336, 346.)

Reading Numbers

The number 3725 is read as *three thousand seven hundred twenty-five*. In it, there are 3 thousands, 7 hundreds, 2 tens, and 5 ones. A number with only ones has only one digit; one with tens has two digits; one with hundreds has three digits; and one with thousands has four digits.

5 ones =	5
2 tens =	20
7 hundreds =	700
3 thousands =	3000

Numbers in Word Form

Third graders continue to learn that numbers in word form can be turned into digits (so seven hundred thirty-nine is written as 739).

Expanded Form

To relate the expanded form to its equivalent:

5000 + 300 + 70 + 4 = **5374**

2861 = **2000 + 800 + 60 + 1**

4000 + 30 + 7 = **4037**. There are no hundreds in this expanded form. This must be accounted for.

Writing from Words

"One hundred seven" is written as **107**, not **17**. (It's important that your child notices there's nothing in the tens place.)

Manipulatives

Most classrooms work with place value by using manipulative materials. These are often base ten blocks or rods. Blocks are pictured so that the units are in accurate proportion to each other: The *ten* is ten times bigger than the *one* (the *ten* is the same as 10 *ones* glued side by side). Your child should be able to look at a picture of a group of manipulatives and write the corresponding number.

Understanding place value and numbers as a prescribed sequence allows your child to be able to determine whether numbers are *greater than* or *less than* each other. In addition, your child has been introduced to the symbols used to denote greater than and less than.

427 > 136 four hundred twenty-seven is *greater than* one hundred thirty-six

337 < 584 three hundred thirty-seven is *less than* five hundred eighty-four

---

TIP

To help your child remember which symbol is which, make them meaningful. Have your child think of the symbols as the mouth of an alligator. The alligator is always hungry, therefore it will seek out the larger number. Thus, the mouth of the alligator always faces the larger number.

Properties

Numbers can be *odd* or *even*. If a number is even, it can be separated into two equal groups. Four is even because it can be separated into two groups of two; eight is even because it can be separated into two groups of four. An odd number cannot be separated into two equal groups.

As your child learns the basic math facts, he is introduced to several basic mathematical properties. First, the addends in an addition problem can be switched without affecting the sum, or the answer. Thus, 3 + 4 is the same as 4 + 3. They both equal 7. Second, both sides of the equal sign need to be equal in value (3 + 5 = 2 + 6). Third, the basic operations have an inverse relationship. 4 + 9 = 13; therefore, 13 − 9 = 4.

What You and Your Child Can Do

Numbers are all around us. No matter which concept you are working on, have your child come up with real examples. Making the concept real is likely to enhance learning.

Make a Number Grid. Using a piece of graph paper (preferably ½-inch by ½-inch squares), have your child make a grid 10 squares by 10 squares and fill in all of the numbers. Have your child make ten of these, with the next one beginning where the previous one left off. Your child will then have a string of grids whose numbers go from one to 1000. Do any patterns emerge?

Use these grids for skip counting. Take a set of same-colored chips and cover every tenth number. Have your child look at the pattern. Have your child write down the sequence (every number that was covered); what pattern emerges? Cover every second number, or every fifth number, for example. Does a different pattern emerge? Let your child be a detective to see what can be determined.

Number Mysteries. Using the number grid, trace a section of numbers in which the shape isn't a uniform square or rectangle. Copy only one of the numbers, then give the incomplete shape to your child. Have her fill in the mystery numbers. This helps your child with skip counting. The number directly below is +10, the number directly to the right is +1, the number directly to the left is –1, the number directly above is –10.

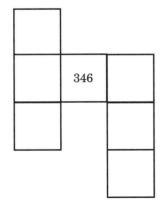

Leap Frog. Decide on a number for skip counting and a starting number. Draw several lily pads in a row, with a number written on one of the lily pads. Vary which pad you put the number on. Your child is to use the skip count amount to fill in the missing numbers on the other lily pads. Make these more difficult by having the skip count cross a hundred, thereby requiring your child to change two of the digits.

Patterns. Beginning early in their school careers, students are exposed to patterns, often starting with patterns in shapes or colors and then moving to patterns in number sequences. The reverse of **Leap Frog** is to present your child with a number pattern in which one or more numbers are omitted. Your child is to determine the pattern, then supply the missing numbers.

3 7 11 15 ___ ___

The pattern above is skip counting by 4; therefore, the next two numbers are *19* and *23*. You can make the missing numbers occur anywhere in the pattern, as long as you include two successive numbers from which your child can determine the pattern.

5 11 ___ 23 ___   (17, 29)
pattern: +6

___ 248 251 ___ 257   (245, 254)
pattern: +3

Make Up Riddles. Make up a riddle about a number and have your child guess it. For example, "I have four digits, a three in the tens place, and I am less than 1459." Notice that there are many numbers that will be correct (for example, 1439, 1337, 1030). How many can your child think of?

Make the riddles more complex. "I have three digits, and two of my digits add up to nine." (Correct answers include 458, 630, 900, 183.)

Newspaper Activities. Have your child search the newspaper or a magazine looking for advertisements that include prices.

Have your child cut out five numbers and order them from smallest to largest, or largest to smallest. Have your child read them to you.

Look at a page with several ads on it. You read a number out loud and have your child find it on the page.

You can also use the sports page, which is filled with scores. Have your child compare various teams based on the score of their games. Make up challenge questions such as, Which combination of two basketball teams would have the most points? Telling your child not to worry about the decimal points, you can ask which baseball player has the lowest ERA. Who has the second lowest ERA? How much lower? How much separates the highest and the lowest?

Practice, Practice. Write down ten numbers on a page: two-, three-, and four-digit numbers. Have your child read each number. Then ask for the value of one of the digits within each number.

> 7159 read as "seven thousand one hundred fifty-nine."
>
> *What value does the 5 have?* "It is 5 tens."
>
> *How much does that equal?* "50."

Have your child write the number in expanded form: 7000 + 100 + 50 + 9.

Present a number in expanded form and have your child write its equivalent, then read it.

> 600 + 70 + 3 equals 673 "Six hundred seventy-three."

To make these challenging, leave out a place value:

> 4000 + 50 + 3 equals 4053 NOT 453

Manipulatives. Make your own manipulatives to help your child understand the concept of place value. Use straws or popsicle sticks to create ones, tens, hundreds, and thousands. One popsicle stick is a *one*, ten sticks tied with a rubber band is a *ten*, ten bundles of ten tied together is a *hundred*.

Make about 15 of each unit for your child to work with; this will enable you to use the manipulatives when you work with computation in Chapter 7.

After you have made the manipulatives, present a grouping of ones, tens, and hundreds. Have your child state, then write, the corresponding number. Make sure you present less than 10 of each unit.

The amount of practice your child needs on each of these concepts will depend on how comfortable your child is with that concept. If she can answer questions easily, don't continue with extensive practice. Move to an area in which she is not so strong. (However, to ensure that your child understands the earlier, less difficult concept, ask her to do a problem in a few days, without providing any review or special introduction. Present it cold. If your child can do it accurately, without difficulty, on several different presentations spread out over time, then your child has likely mastered the concept.)

Practice Skill: Math Concepts

Directions: Choose the number that belongs in the blank.

1 18   20   22   24   _____
- (A) 25
- (B) 26
- (C) 28
- (D) 30

---

2 436   446   _____   466
- (A) 426
- (B) 450
- (C) 456
- (D) 465

---

3 1853 _____ 1859 1862
1865

- Ⓐ 1854
- Ⓑ 1855
- Ⓒ 1856
- Ⓓ 1857

Directions: What is the value of the underlined number?

4 4<u>7</u>6

- Ⓐ 7
- Ⓑ 70
- Ⓒ 700
- Ⓓ 76

5 <u>2</u>369

- Ⓐ 2
- Ⓑ 20
- Ⓒ 200
- Ⓓ 2000

6 <u>5</u>31

- Ⓐ 5000
- Ⓑ 5300
- Ⓒ 500
- Ⓓ 5

7 What number is **5321**?

- Ⓐ five hundred twenty-one
- Ⓑ five thousand three hundred twenty-one
- Ⓒ fifty-three thousand twenty-one
- Ⓓ five thousand three hundred twelve

8 600 + 30 + 7 = what number?

- Ⓐ 637
- Ⓑ 6307
- Ⓒ 673
- Ⓓ 60037

9 Three thousand two hundred six is what number?

- Ⓐ 326
- Ⓑ 32006
- Ⓒ 30026
- Ⓓ 3206

Directions: Put these numbers in order, from largest to smallest.

10 4380 4169 4271 4954

- Ⓐ 4169 4380 4271 4954
- Ⓑ 4954 4169 4380 4271
- Ⓒ 4169 4271 4380 4954
- Ⓓ 4954 4380 4271 4169

11 What number belongs in the blank?

$$4 + 9 = 6 + \_\_\_\_$$

- Ⓐ 5
- Ⓑ 6
- Ⓒ 7
- Ⓓ 8

12 What number belongs in the blank?

$$476 > \_\_\_\_$$

- Ⓐ 474
- Ⓑ 479
- Ⓒ 482
- Ⓓ 497

(See pages 99–100 for answer key.)

CHAPTER 7

Math Computation

In this chapter we review the computation skills your child has been learning. Up to now, your child has probably worked mostly with addition and subtraction. During third grade these will continue and your child will develop a conceptual understanding of multiplication and division. All four of these operations are presented.

What Your Third Grader Should Be Learning

By the time your child reaches third grade, he will have spent much time developing a sound understanding of addition and subtraction, with a focus on maintaining accuracy. This work is then expanded to addition and subtraction with multi-digit numbers, and regrouping when necessary. Third grade is also a time to develop a conceptual understanding of multiplication and division. Depending on your child's school and his particular level of achievement, he may be introduced to multiplication with multi-digit numbers.

What Tests May Ask

The skills within this chapter appear on standardized tests both as problems presented in isolation and as word problems. Working with word problems is also discussed in Chapter 8.

Addition

Your child should be comfortable with the basic facts and understand that addition is the same as *combining groups*; the sum (answer) is always larger than either of the two groups individually.

Multi-Digit Numbers

After the curriculum within the elementary school develops your child's understanding of place value, addition of multi-digit numbers is introduced. At first, numbers are added in each column, with the sum always less than 10. This is addition without regrouping.

$$\begin{array}{r} 45 \\ + \ 23 \\ \hline \end{array}$$

Help your child understand that you always start with the ones column and then add the tens column. This makes adding with regrouping an easier task.

$$\begin{array}{cc} \text{Step 1:} & \text{Step 2:} \\ \begin{array}{r} 45 \\ + \ 23 \\ \hline 8 \end{array} & \begin{array}{r} 45 \\ + \ 23 \\ \hline 68 \end{array} \end{array}$$

Once your child understands this concept, he can add any size multi-digit number. Children often express delight that they can solve problems such as this one.

$$\begin{array}{r} 2581940217264893176 \\ + \ 1417031562612004521 \\ \hline \end{array}$$

Multi-Number Problems

In addition to multi-digit numbers, have your child practice adding more than two numbers at one time. Again, the concept is the same; you start with the ones column.

$$
\begin{array}{r}
244 \\
321 \\
+\ 123 \\
\end{array}
$$

Make up problems using a mixture of some numbers having hundreds and some having tens. This reinforces the concept of adding within a column.

$$
\begin{array}{r}
502 \\
25 \\
+\ 132 \\
\end{array}
$$

TIP

If your child is having difficulty following the columns, present the problems on graph paper. Once he develops this skill, take the graph paper away. If your child continues to have difficulty following the columns, strategies such as placing a lightly drawn line across each number as it is added or placing a small dot above each number as it is added may help.

Regrouping

After your child becomes comfortable with addition without regrouping, regrouping is introduced. Regrouping occurs when the sum of the addends in a particular column is greater than 10.

$$
\begin{array}{r}
68 \\
+\ 19 \\
\end{array}
$$

In the above problem, if you add the ones column, you get 17. However, 17 has two digits and there is only one slot. If we remember place value, 17 equals 10 (a ten stick) + 7 (7 one units). Given this, the ten in 17 can be carried over to the tens column, which leaves 7 ones.

$$
\begin{array}{cc}
\text{Step 1:} & \text{Step 2:} \\
1 & 1 \\
68 & 68 \\
+\ 19 & +\ 19 \\
\hline
7 & 87 \\
\end{array}
$$

One way to help explain this is to describe the procedure as *going to the bank*. If the sum of the ones column is 10 or greater, you go to the bank and exchange ten ones for a ten stick. If your child is having difficulty with this concept, use the manipulatives and have your child actually make the exchange, so he can see that he now has fewer ones, but more tens. Make sure your child recognizes that the value of the number is constant; the form has changed but not the overall value.

Give your child lots of practice with two-digit regrouping until the procedure is completed without hesitation. Once your child understands the concept, it is applied to larger numbers. The following progression outlines the various applications.

Three-digit numbers, with regrouping in the ones place:

$$
\begin{array}{r}
136 \\
+\ 328 \\
\end{array}
$$

Three-digit numbers, with regrouping in the tens place:

$$
\begin{array}{r}
352 \\
+\ 584 \\
\end{array}
$$

Three-digit numbers, with regrouping in the ones <u>and</u> the tens places:

$$
\begin{array}{r}
289 \\
+\ 137 \\
\end{array}
$$

By providing a mixture of problems, you can make sure that your child understands the concept and isn't just following a rote procedure. The child who carries when not required to has memorized a procedure without understanding the concept behind it.

Look at the mistakes your child is making. Is she making computation errors, but using the correct procedure? Is he adding correctly, yet not following the correct procedure?

These problems contain computation errors:

1	1	1
37	54	59
+ 28	+ 29	+ 15
64	93	75
7 + 8 = 14	1 + 5 + 2 = 9	9 + 5 = 15

The following problems contain procedural errors:

A
$$\begin{array}{r} 1 \\ 329 \\ + 137 \\ \hline 556 \end{array}$$

B
$$\begin{array}{r} 56 \\ + 28 \\ \hline 714 \end{array}$$

C
$$\begin{array}{r} 1\ 1 \\ 286 \\ 27 \\ + 132 \\ \hline 645 \end{array}$$

In Problem A, the student recognized that regrouping was necessary for the ones, but placed the regrouping number in the hundreds column, not the tens.

In Problem B, the student didn't regroup, but placed the sum of the ones column (a two-digit number) in the tens and ones columns.

In Problem C, the student counted the 2 in 27 as a ten and as a hundred, thereby not following the columns.

If you aren't sure how your child arrived at a particular answer, have him explain to you what he did. Then you can identify where the mistake is occurring.

How you help your child depends on the type of error he's making. In the first set of errors, he needs to continue to practice the math facts. In the second set, a review of the concept (using manipulatives) is needed.

Practice Skill: Addition

Directions: Choose the correct answer for each problem.

1
$$\begin{array}{r} 26 \\ + 42 \end{array}$$

Ⓐ 65
Ⓑ 68
Ⓒ 75
Ⓓ 88

2
$$\begin{array}{r} 3681 \\ + 2207 \end{array}$$

Ⓐ 6777
Ⓑ 5876
Ⓒ 5888
Ⓓ 4888

3
$$\begin{array}{r} 49 \\ + 38 \end{array}$$

Ⓐ 88
Ⓑ 86
Ⓒ 78
Ⓓ 87

4   146
   + 482

     (A)   628
     (B)   637
     (C)   528
     (D)   537

5   143
   + 426

     (A)   568
     (B)   658
     (C)   569
     (D)   566

(See page 100 for answer key.)

Subtraction

Your child should be able to easily handle the basic subtraction facts. In addition, he should have a solid understanding of subtraction as *starting with a larger group from which a part is taken away*; the answer is always smaller than the starting number.

After the curriculum within the elementary school develops your child's understanding of place value, subtraction of multi-digit numbers is introduced. At first, numbers are subtracted in each column, with the answer always less than 10. This is subtraction without regrouping:

$$26 \\ -\,14$$

Again, help your child understand that you always start with the ones and then subtract the tens. This makes subtraction with regrouping an easier task.

Step 1:	Step 2:
26	26
− 14	− 14
2	12

Once your child understands this concept, he can subtract any size multi-digit number. As with addition, children often express delight that they can solve problems such as this one:

$$5582948217669847296 \\ -\,1411031012612304121$$

Note: Make sure your child can subtract multi-digit numbers, without regrouping, when the answer in a particular column is zero. It is important that he recognize the need to write the zero within the problem.

> **TIP**
>
> **If your child is having trouble following the columns, present the problems on graph paper. Once he develops this skill, take the graph paper away.**

After your child can accurately subtract simple numbers, the teacher will introduce regrouping. Regrouping occurs when the ones to be subtracted are greater than the ones in the starting number.

$$56 \\ -\,19$$

In the above problem, you start in the ones column and subtract 9 from 6. However, this can't be done: 9 is larger than 6, so you don't have enough ones. But because 56 is larger than 19, the problem is doable. Help your child recognize this.

Use the manipulatives if he is having difficulty with this concept. Give your child 5 tens and 6 ones. Ask him to give you 19. Let your child try to come up with a solution, which is to trade in one of the 5 tens and get 10 ones in return. This then leaves you with only 4 tens but 16 ones, as noted in step one below.

After the regrouping has been carried out,

you're ready to subtract. Start with the ones column: 16 – 9 equals 7, so 7 is written in the ones column, as seen in step two. Step three shows completion of the problem: Subtract the tens column.

Step 1

```
 4 16
 5 6
– 19
```

Step 2

```
 4 16
 5 6
– 19
   7
```

Step 3

```
 4 16
 5 6
– 19
  37
```

As with addition, one way to help explain this is to describe the procedure as *going to the bank*. If you don't have enough ones, go to the bank and exchange a ten for ten ones. If your child has trouble with this concept, use the manipulatives and have your child actually make the exchange, so he can see that he now has fewer tens but more ones. Help your child recognize that the actual value of the number has not changed; it is just in a different form.

Give your child lots of practice with two-digit regrouping until the procedure is completed without hesitation. Once your child understands the concept, it is applied to larger numbers. The following progression outlines the various applications:

Three-digit numbers, with regrouping in the ones place:

```
 586
–328
```

Three-digit numbers, with regrouping in the tens place:

```
 859
–584
```

Regrouping with a zero:

```
 204        100
– 19       – 26
```

Mixing Problems

As with addition, presenting a mixture of problems helps you ensure that your child understands the concept and isn't just following a rote procedure. *The child who regroups when not required to or who fails to regroup has memorized a procedure without understanding the concept behind it.*

Look at the mistakes your child is making. Is he making computation errors, but using the correct procedure? Are the errors occurring in the procedure, but he is adding correctly?

Help your child recognize that he can check his answer by adding:

```
  453        317
– 136       + 136
  317        453
```

Make sure your child is actually crossing out the number when regrouping, and writing the new number above it. Mistakes are often made when a child tries to carry out the process in his head.

Computation errors:

```
  4 17          2 14          8 13
  5 7           3 4           9 3
– 38          – 29          – 65
  11            45            15

17 – 8 = 1    2 – 2 = 4    13 – 5 = 5
                           8 – 6 = 1
```

Procedural errors:

A   361
        − 137
         236

B   4 17
        $\not5\not6$
        − 19
         38

C   18
         4$\not8$
        − 29
         29

In Problem A, the student did not recognize that regrouping was necessary for the ones.

In Problem B, the student recognized the need to regroup, but added a one and a ten to the 6, thereby getting 17.

In Problem C, the student forgot to regroup the tens in order to be able to subtract the ones.

As with addition, how you help your child depends on the type of error being made. For computation errors, the student needs to continue to practice the math facts. For procedural errors, he needs to review the concept using manipulatives.

TIP

To enhance learning of the math facts, present them as facts families.

3, 4, 7

Within the family of "3, 4, 7" four math facts can be generated:

3 + 4 = 7   7 − 3 = 4
4 + 3 = 7   7 − 4 = 3

Practice Skill: Subtraction

Directions: Choose the correct answer for each problem.

6   94
        − 33
- (A) 127   (B) 61
- (C) 67   (D) 51

7   76
        − 27
- (A) 49   (B) 43
- (C) 103   (D) 39

8   686
        − 134
- (A) 551   (B) 553
- (C) 552   (D) 550

9   493
        − 188
- (A) 311   (B) 411
- (C) 501   (D) 305

(See page 100 for answer key.)

Multiplication

When presented with the concept of multiplication, students learn that sets of equal amounts are combined. Multiplication is similar to repeated addition.

★★★★   2 sets of 4 stars
★★★★   4 + 4
              2 × 4 = 8

●●●●●●   3 sets of 6 marbles
●●●●●●   6 + 6 + 6
●●●●●●   3 × 6 = 18

Your child should understand the concept of multiplication and be able to solve some of the basic facts. Skip counting by twos, fives, and tens allows your child to be able to generate the 2, 5, and 10 times tables.

Multi-Digit Multiplication

Some schools begin to introduce multi-digit multiplication in third grade.

$$34 \quad \text{2 digit number}$$
$$\times 2 \quad \text{multiplier}$$

The progression, as with addition and subtraction, is first to introduce the concept without any carrying across place values, as in the problem above. First the multiplier and the digit in the ones column are multiplied, with the answer placed in the ones column. Then the multiplier and the digit in the tens column are multiplied, with the answer placed in the tens column.

Step 1	Step 2
34	34
× 2	× 2
8	68

When students develop facility with this, multiplication with regrouping is introduced.

$$24$$
$$\times 3$$

The same procedure is followed: In step 1, the multiplier and the digit in the ones column are multiplied (4×3). This equals 12, which is 1 ten and 2 ones. The 2 (for the ones) is placed in the ones column, and the 1 is carried to the tens column (step 1).

Step 1	Step 2 and Step 3
1	1
24	24
× 3	× 3
2	72

Step 2: The multiplier and the digit in the tens column are multiplied (2×3). This equals 6.

Step 3: Add the carried number to the answer in step 2 ($6 + 1 = 7$), and place the answer in the tens column.

Practice Skill: Multiplication

Directions: Choose the correct answer for each question.

10 $4 \times 6 =$
- (A) 20
- (B) 24
- (C) 18
- (D) 30

11 $5 \times 7 =$
- (A) 35
- (B) 30
- (C) 42
- (D) 54

12 21
$\times 3$
- (A) 61
- (B) 93
- (C) 91
- (D) 63

13 $10 \times 4 =$
- (A) 4
- (B) 40
- (C) 41
- (D) 104

14 86
$\times 3$
- (A) 248
- (B) 246
- (C) 426
- (D) 258

(See page 100 for answer key.)

Division

In third grade, when only the concept of division will likely be introduced, your child will be expected to solve basic facts. Division is the opposite of multiplication, just as subtraction is the opposite of addition. You start with a large group of objects, and then separate the group into sets of objects, with the number in each set being constant. The answer is the number of sets you end up with.

In the picture, we start with 27 stars. Groups of 3 are made. That gives us 9 groups.

$$27 \div 3 = 9$$

Your child should understand the concept of division. Moreover, he should recognize the two symbols used to denote division: $\div$ **and** $\overline{)}$. Recognizing that division is the opposite of multiplication will make the process easier to understand.

TIP

Help your child recognize fact families.

3, 7, 21

| $3 \times 7 = 21$ | $21 \div 7 = 3$ |
| $7 \times 3 = 21$ | $21 \div 3 = 7$ |

What You and Your Child Can Do

Review the sample problems within this chapter. Make sure your child can explain how he arrived at the answers. Use the manipulatives discussed previously to enhance your child's understanding of any difficult concepts, and then make up similar problems for your child to complete. Keep practicing until your child understands the concept (or practice with the basic facts, if that is where the difficulty lies).

Make It Meaningful. Math is all around us.

1. Have your child find examples of multiplication and division within your house. For example, windows with panes can become a multiplication problem:

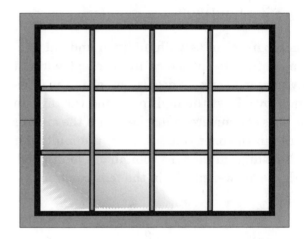

$$3 \times 4 = 12$$

Have your child draw what was found and write the corresponding number equation.

2. Present math word problems as they arise in daily activities.

   The mom in a family of five might ask, as she is preparing dessert:

   "I have 3 pieces of pie cut. How many more do I need?"

Mystery Number. Have your child give you a number less than 20. You perform an operation with that number (for example, add 5). See how many numbers your child must give you before he can figure out what you are doing. (You must perform the same procedure each time.) Make sure you give your child practice, using different games, with all four operations.

Diagrams. Give your child a word problem for a basic fact. Have your child draw a corresponding picture: I have 18 cookies. If I have 6 children, how many cookies will each child get?

Now do the opposite: Give your child a diagram and have him make up a corresponding word problem.

(Example word problem for this diagram: There are three bags of marbles. Each bag has three marbles in it. How many marbles are there in all?)

Mystery Operation. Give your child a word problem. Have her guess the operation.

MOM: I got 27 pieces of candy on Halloween. I ate 10 of them. How many do I have left?

CHILD: Subtraction.

Practice Basic Facts

Flash Cards. Make a game out of it. See how many your child gets correct in one minute. Keep a chart so your child can watch the number correct grow with practice.

Word Value Chart. Write out the alphabet and give each letter a value less than 10. Then write a word. Have your child add up the value of the word, using the alphabet chart. What is the smallest word he can think of that has the largest value? Have your child add up the value of his spelling words. Which word has the largest value?

Practice Skill: Division

Directions: Choose the correct answer for each question.

15 $12 \div 4 =$

Ⓐ 4
Ⓑ 1
Ⓒ 3
Ⓓ 2

16 $9 \div 3 =$

Ⓐ 3
Ⓑ 6
Ⓒ 2
Ⓓ 27

17 $4 \overline{)16}$

Ⓐ 2
Ⓑ 24
Ⓒ 4
Ⓓ 8

(See page 100 for answer key.)

CHAPTER 8

Math Applications

This chapter covers those additional areas that are important for developing a solid foundation in math. Although your child's teacher may not spend much time on math applications, they are still essential for success.

What Your Third Grader Should Be Learning

Third graders are working to develop a solid understanding of the concept of time, which includes being able to read a clock accurately, understand time phrases (such as "half past") and comprehend time equivalents. Your child is also developing a conceptual understanding of fractions and learning more about money equivalents and making change. In addition, concepts associated with geometry and with interpreting data are introduced in third grade.

What Tests May Ask

Standardized tests assess a student's understanding of skills in geometry, money, time, and so on, both in pictorial form and in word problems.

Time

By third grade, your child has been exposed to the concepts associated with telling time for several years and is now learning to tell time to the minute. (That is, looking at a clock and stating that it is 6:48.) In addition, your child is being asked to work with alternative phrases about the time, such as quarter after (4:15); quarter to (3:45); and half past (4:30). She is also working with time equivalents; that is, that 60 seconds = 1 minute; 30 minutes = 1/2 hour; 60 minutes = 1 hour; and 24 hours = 1 day.

What You and Your Child Can Do

Tell Time. Make sure you have an analog clock somewhere in the house. In the days of increased technology, many of our clocks are digital. Although they are easier to read, they don't provide opportunities for your child to practice.

If you don't have an analog clock, you can make one out of a paper plate. Draw the numbers 1 to 12 evenly around the plate to designate the hours, then make small lines on the perimeter to designate the minutes. Have your child draw two thick arrows, one shorter than the other, and attach these to the center of the plate with a fastener. Use of the fastener makes it possible to move the arrows so you can designate different times for your child to work with.

Be sure to have your child practice telling the time **and** practice using the hands on the clock to show the time that you state.

In addition, have your child practice going from one time to the next. For example, ask your child to show you 7:05. Then ask your child to show you the time 25 minutes later; have her then name that time. After your child is able to do this when the hour doesn't change, have her try it when adding time makes the hour change. (Show 7:45. Show 20 minutes later. New time: 8:05.) This is a more advanced skill; it may be difficult for your child and may require extra practice.

Use Riddles. You can provide additional practice by taking advantage of opportunities in your everyday life. When your child asks you a question related to time, put the answer in riddle form.

CHILD: Mom, when are we going to the store?

MOM: We're leaving 15 minutes before 4 o'clock. What time is that?

CHILD: That's 3:45.

Practice Duplicates. Many times have more than one name. For example, 4:15 can be called "four fifteen." It can also be called "a quarter after four" and "fifteen minutes after four." Pick a time. Have your child generate as many names as possible. Which times have the most names?

Money

As with time, the concept of money has been presented within the curriculum over the past few years, with each exposure presenting new skills. In third grade, your child will be expected to recognize and know the value of coins, know coin equivalencies, know how to read money in written form ($2.45), and know how to make change.

EQUIVALENTS TO KNOW

pennies:	in a nickel (5), dime (10), quarter (25), half dollar (50), dollar (100)
nickels:	in a dime (2), quarter (5), half dollar (10), dollar (20)
dimes:	in a half dollar (5), a dollar (10)
quarters:	in a half dollar (2), a dollar (4)
half dollar:	in a dollar (2)
dollars:	in a five dollar bill (5), ten dollar bill (10)

What You and Your Child Can Do

Because standardized tests aren't given out loud, your child needs to be familiar with the written form of an amount of money as well as with the visual image of coins. Therefore, when you practice, make sure you or your child is writing down the amount; make sure you use coins to show the amount.

Exposure. Gather a pile of coins. Take a portion of them and have your child add up the value. Put that portion back and have your child take another portion. How much is that worth?

Make a game out of it: What is the most money your child can grab at one time, with one hand?

Allowance. If you give your child a weekly allowance, instead of giving the amount in its most efficient form, present it using different mixtures of coins. Have your child add the amount to make sure you gave the correct amount. Alternatively, give your child too much and ask for change.

Store. Some third graders still enjoy playing store. This provides an excellent opportunity to work with money. Have your child gather various items and give them prices. One person is the shopper and the other the store owner. Did the shopper give enough money to pay for the purchases? Is the change given the correct amount?

Even if your child is no longer interested in playing store, have your child pay for something when you are actually making a purchase. Let your child tell you the amount it sells for, gather the money from your wallet to pay for it, and then make sure the clerk gave the correct change.

Eating Out. If you go to a restaurant, you have an excellent opportunity to practice with money. The menu provides the means to ask many questions. What could you buy if you had $5? Which item costs the most money? Which item costs the least money?

Riddles. Make up riddles about coin equivalencies. Would you rather have 10 nickels or 20 pennies? Have your child use real money to figure it out as needed.

Fractions

The introduction of fractions into the curriculum presents the student with a different way to understand numbers. She now needs to take a whole and split it into parts.

Your child should understand the pictorial representation of a fraction, be familiar with the relationship between basic fractions in terms of their size (1/2 > 1/3 > 1/4), and understand the difference between the numerator and the denominator so she can write the fraction associated with a pictorial representation.

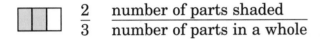 $\dfrac{2}{3}$ $\dfrac{\text{number of parts shaded}}{\text{number of parts in a whole}}$

What You and Your Child Can Do

In the Kitchen. Cooking and eating present many opportunities to work with fractions. We can cut a pie into quarters. We cut a sandwich in half. We use a quarter of a cup of sugar.

As you cook and eat, look for opportunities to share fractions with your child. Have your child measure out the half cup of sugar. Have your child cut the pie into quarters. Ask your child which ingredient was greater in quantity, the half cup of sugar or the quarter cup of oil.

Around the House. Examples of fractions are all around the house. Have your child look for things that are divided into equal parts, then draw them. After that's done, have your child color in a fraction of that object, using the natural dividers. For example, a closet with sliding doors has two parts; if your child colors one, she has shaded one-half. Have your child label the fraction. You can have your child sort the pictures and determine which fraction had the most examples.

Interpreting Data

Throughout the math curriculum, your child has been exposed to information in symbolic form. In addition to more straightforward math problems, your child's developing cognitive skills allow her to interpret information when it's presented in bar graphs, charts, and calendars.

Bar graphs, as a way to tally information, are often seen in the classroom. The *number of teeth lost, number of books read,* or *number of sunny days* all offer opportunities to make bar graphs.

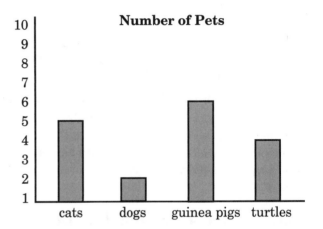

When reading bar graphs, your child is often making comparisons. For example, in the graph of pets, your child can determine which kind of pet is most popular. Similarly, having increased facility with numbers, your child can determine how many more turtles are pets than dogs.

Charts also offer a way to interpret information. In a chart, information is presented in several columns. This information is then used to make comparisons.

Type of book	Number read
mysteries	26
poems	13
animal stories	42
historical fiction	37

In this chart, the information can be used to make comparisons between the types of books read. Questions you may ask are: Which type of book was read the most? The least? How many books were read in all?

Calendars are a third source of information your child is learning to interpret.

			March			
Sun	Mon	Tues	Wed	Thurs	Fri	Sat
	1	2	3	4	5	6
7	8	9	10	11	12	13
14	15	16	17	18	19	20
21	22	23	24	25	26	27
28	29	30	31			

In third grade, your child will be asked to tell the days of the week, in order, knowing that Sunday is the first day, to tell what day of the week a certain day is (March 23 is a Tuesday, the first Saturday is March 6), and to be able to figure out what day of the week a set number of days from a specified date will fall (six days from March 13 will be on a Friday).

What You and Your Child Can Do

Bar graphs can easily be put in place in the home. For example, when practicing math facts, use a bar graph to tally progress. Keep track of which toys were played with each day, then make comparisons at the end of the week.

Charts can be made for household activities. Select several favorite computer games. Keep track of how many times each was played in a week. Turn this into a chart by adding up the tallies.

Computer game	Number of times played

If you use a chart that lists chores to be done each week, have your child turn it into a chart with numbers. Although the numbers may be small, your child will still get practice with the concept of reading charts.

Julie's Chore Chart

Sun	Mon	Tues	Wed	Thur	Fri	Sat
trash	make bed	recycle	trash	make bed		make bed
make bed		make bed		make bed		make bed
		set table	set table		set table	
rake leaves						

Day of the week	Number of chores
Sunday	3
Monday	1
Tuesday	3
Wednesday	2
Thursday	2
Friday	1
Saturday	2

Ask questions: Which days have the fewest chores? The most chores? The same number of chores? How many chores does Julie do in one week? If Julie did chores for 3 weeks, how many would she do in all? As a review, you can ask: What operation did you use to solve that?

Have your child try to determine topics for a chart. Making her own chart is a good way for her to show her understanding of the concept.

You probably have plenty of calendars. Use the lunch menu from school or a master calendar that lists scheduled activities to ask questions such as: Which day of the week has the most organized activities? On which day of the week do we have the fewest organized activities? How many more days until Susie's birthday party? On which day of the week is pizza served? If it is November 13, how many more days until the school is serving hamburgers for lunch?

Geometry

Geometry is the part of math that deals with measurement, properties of shapes, and relationships between shapes. You'll find that geometry is all around us and can easily be applied to real-life situations.

Measurement

By third grade, your child will have measured many objects. At first, objects are measured using nonstandard units. For example, given a book and a string of paper clips along one side, your child might have answered the question: About how many paper clips long is this book?

Now that she is developing cognitive skills, your child is able to measure in standard units that allow comparison across objects. These standard units are inches and centimeters. Using a ruler, your child is learning to measure the length of both a single straight line and a straight line that changes directions. The latter skill is important for being able to measure the perimeter of an object.

Your child should be aware of several terms used with measurement, including *perimeter, line segment,* and *closed figure.* She should understand that objects can be inside or outside a figure. In addition to measuring, your child will be developing her understanding of equivalencies (12 inches = 1 foot) and learning that different properties, besides length, can be measured (weight = pounds, volume = pint, quart). Some schools also present volume and weight in the metric system.

Shapes

By third grade, your child has likely been exposed to various shapes many times. In addition to recognizing the different shapes, your child is learning to identify, using appropriate terminology, the properties of a square, rectangle, triangle, and circle. (For example, a circle has no sides and no corners.) Third graders are also introduced to three-dimensional shapes (cube, cylinder), with focus on recognizing their properties: The cube has squares on the sides; the cylinder has circles on the ends.

With the development of cognitive skills, third graders can now find two objects with the same shape but different sizes, and they can find two objects with the same perimeter, but different shapes.

What You and Your Child Can Do

Go on a Shape Hunt. Have your child look for shapes around the house. Make a bar graph or chart to show how many were found. Windows are rectangles, lamp shades are circles, and glasses become cylinders. Have your child find objects that are the same shape but different sizes. How many different size triangles can she find? Are there more squares of differing sizes or more rectangles?

Graphing. Using graph paper, have your child experiment with different problem situations. Have her draw something and then measure its perimeter. See if she can then draw a different shape that has the same perimeter. Have your child draw a shape. See if she can then draw the same shape, but in a different size.

Have your child write a word in block letters on the graph paper, then add up the perimeter. Have your child make comparisons: Which letter has the largest perimeter? The smallest? What is the shortest word she can think of that has the largest perimeter? What is the longest word with the shortest perimeter?

Word Problems

Word problems present mathematical procedures in story form. In order to be successful, your child needs to understand what the story is asking for and then be able to carry out the mathematical procedure correctly. To help your child with word problems, first make sure your child has a sound conceptual understanding of the basic mathematical procedures: addition, subtraction, multiplication, and division. Then help your child learn to look for "buzz" words that designate the procedure.

For addition, look for phrases such as How many in all? or How many all together? Subtraction deals with what is remaining, as in, How many are left? Things that were "lost," "given away," or "eaten" all signal that something was removed and only a portion remains. Subtraction may also be used in the comparison of two groups (How many more? How many less?). In multiplication, sets of equal size are combined. Because multiplication can be solved as repeated addition, the buzz words are similar. The characteristics of the groups being combined designate whether multiplication is a viable solution. For example, three bags of six cookies could be either addition or multiplication, but three apples and four apples can only be addition because the sets are unequal. In division, sets of equal amount are separated from a large group: How many did *each* person get?

What You and Your Child Can Do

Practice, Practice, Practice. As noted in Chapter 7, you can start with word problems using the basic facts. As your child becomes more proficient at determining the correct operation, make the numbers larger and have your child use paper and pencil to solve the problems.

When situations occur in your everyday life that are in essence word problems, have your child help you solve them. For example, suppose your child is having a birthday party and 17 children are invited. If everyone is to get 3 treats in the goody bag, how many treats do you need to buy in all?

Give your child a challenge word problem every day, or have your child give you a challenge word problem. Make a mistake every once in a while. Your child needs to answer the question in order to tell you whether your answer is correct.

Make sure the problem and answer are written down so your child can *see* the correct equations. Standardized tests are all visual. Your child needs to identify the correct answer or identify the correct equation out of the choices presented.

Challenge Word Problems

Standardized tests include word problems in which the problem can't be solved because not enough information is given. Your child needs to be able to recognize this.

Having a sound conceptual understanding of each operation will help your child determine when these types of problems are presented. In addition, have your child write down the number equation corresponding to the word problem, using a question mark to designate what is being solved for. Missing numbers will signal that not enough information is given.

Addition: _____ + _____ = _?_

Susie has 6 balls and Jill has some. How many do they have all together?

_6_	+	don't know	=	_?_
Susie		Jill		

The number of balls Jill has is not given; therefore this problem cannot be solved.

Subtraction: _____ – _____ = _?_

Barbara had 24 Beanie Babies. Some of them were bears and some were cats.

How many bears did she have?

_24_ –	–	don't know	=	_?_
total		not bears		bears
Beanie Babies				

Multiplication: _____ × _____ = _?_

Tom has 6 bags of marbles. Each bag has the same number of blue marbles.

How many blue marbles does Tom have in all?

_6_	×	don't know	=	_?_
# of bags		# of blue marbles in each bag		total blue marbles

Division: _____ ÷ _____ = _?_

Ann bought 16 candy bars to give to her friends. She wanted each friend to get the same amount.

How many did each friend get?

$$\underset{\text{Ann's bars}}{\underline{\quad 16 \quad}} \div \underset{\substack{\text{\# of friends}}}{\underline{\text{don't know}}} = \underset{\substack{\text{how} \\ \text{many} \\ \text{each got}}}{\underline{\quad ? \quad}}$$

In addition, word problems can be presented with more information than is needed to solve the problem. The extra information is presented to serve as a distraction. Again, have your child follow the procedure of using only the information that fits the conceptual understanding. For example:

Brian had 36 stamps. He collected stamps from 6 different countries. He gave 14 of the stamps to his friend Tommy. How many stamps did he have left?

Buzz word: <u>have left</u>. The operation is subtraction.

$$\underset{\substack{\text{number of} \\ \text{stamps}}}{\underline{\quad 36 \quad}} - \underset{\substack{\text{given} \\ \text{away}}}{\underline{\quad 14 \quad}} = \underset{\substack{\text{how many} \\ \text{left}}}{\underline{\quad ? \quad}}$$

The information about the 6 countries isn't needed.

Practice Skill: Math Applications

Directions: Choose the correct answer for each problem.

1 Susie has 32 jelly beans. She finds 16 more in a jar. How many jelly beans does she have altogether?

Ⓐ 32 − 16 =
Ⓑ 16 − 32 =
Ⓒ 32 + 16 =
Ⓓ not enough information

2 Lucy made 132 cotton snowmen for a party. She lost 16 of them. How many did she have left?

Ⓐ 132 − 16 =
Ⓑ 132 ÷ 16 =
Ⓒ 132 × 16 =
Ⓓ not enough information

3 Mr. Smith had 36 bananas. He gave the same number to each of his monkeys. How many did each monkey get?

Ⓐ 36 − 9 =
Ⓑ 36 + 9 =
Ⓒ 36 ÷ 9 =
Ⓓ not enough information

4 Mrs. Jones drove 26 miles on Monday and 36 miles on Tuesday. She drove for 3 hours each day. How many miles did she drive altogether?

Ⓐ 26 + 3 + 36 =
Ⓑ 26 + 26 + 36 =
Ⓒ 26 + 36 =
Ⓓ not enough information

5 Bobby and Sam liked to swim. Bobby swam 56 laps. Sam swam 83 laps. How many more laps did Sam swim than Bobby?

Ⓐ 56 + 83 =
Ⓑ 83 − 56 =
Ⓒ 83 ÷ 56 =
Ⓓ not enough information

6 Martha took 29 soft pretzels to school. She gave them to her class. How many did each student get?

   Ⓐ $29 - 1 =$
   Ⓑ $29 - 16 =$
   Ⓒ $29 \div 14 =$
   Ⓓ not enough information

7 John and Robert each have 8 trading cards. How many do they have all together?

   Ⓐ $8 \times 2 =$
   Ⓑ $8 \times 1 =$
   Ⓒ $8 \div 2 =$
   Ⓓ not enough information

8 Sally collects clay animals. She has 36 brown bears and 15 black bears. She also has 9 tigers. How many bears does she have altogether?

   Ⓐ $36 + 15 + 9 =$
   Ⓑ $36 + 15 =$
   Ⓒ $36 + 15 - 9 =$
   Ⓓ not enough information

9 I made 3 trays of cookies. Each tray holds 12 cookies. How many cookies did I make in all?

   Ⓐ $3 \times 12 =$
   Ⓑ $3 + 12 =$
   Ⓒ $3 + 3 + 3 =$
   Ⓓ not enough information

10 George had one bag of marbles. He lost 24 of them. How many did he have left?

   Ⓐ $1 \times 24 =$
   Ⓑ $24 - 36 =$
   Ⓒ $36 - 24 =$
   Ⓓ not enough information

11 Sally went to work at 6:30. She came home 3 hours later. What time did she come home?

   Ⓐ 9:30
   Ⓑ 3:30
   Ⓒ 6:30
   Ⓓ 6:33

12 Michael started his math worksheet at 5:00. It took him a quarter of an hour to finish it. What time did he finish?

   Ⓐ 5:30
   Ⓑ 5:45
   Ⓒ 5:15 ✓
   Ⓓ 9:00

(See page 100 for answer key.)

Web Sites and Resources for More Information

Homework

Homework Central
http://www.HomeworkCentral.com
Terrific site for students, parents, and teachers, filled with information, projects, and more.

Win the Homework Wars
(Sylvan Learning Centers)
http://www.educate.com/online/qa_peters.html

Reading and Grammar Help

Born to Read: How to Raise a Reader
http://www.ala.org/alsc/raise_a_reader.html

Guide to Grammar and Writing
http://webster.commnet.edu/hp/pages/darling/grammar.htm
Help with "plague words and phrases," grammar FAQs, sentence parts, punctuation, rules for common usage.

Internet Public Library: Reading Zone
http://www.ipl.org/cgi-bin/youth/youth.out

Keeping Kids Reading and Writing
http://www.tiac.net/users/maryl/

U.S. Dept. of Education: Helping Your Child Learn to Read
http://www.ed.gov/pubs/parents/Reading/index.html

Math Help

Center for Advancement of Learning
http://www.muskingum.edu/%7Ecal/database/Math2.html
Substitution and memory strategies for math.

Center for Advancement of Learning
http://www.muskingum.edu/%7Ecal/database/Math1.html
General tips and suggestions.

Math.com
http://www.math.com
The world of math online.

Math.com
http://www.math.com/student/testprep.html
Get ready for standardized tests.

Math.com: Homework Help in Math
http://www.math.com/students/homework.html

Math.com: Math for Homeschoolers
http://www.math.com/parents/homeschool.html

The Math Forum: Problems and Puzzles
http://forum.swarthmore.edu/library/resource_types/problems_puzzles
Lots of fun math puzzles and problems for grades K through 12.

The Math Forum: Math Tips and Tricks
http://forum.swarthmore.edu/k12/mathtips/mathtips.html

Tips on Testing

Books on Test Preparation

http://www.testbooksonline.com/preHS.asp
This site provides printed resources for parents who wish to help their children prepare for standardized school tests.

Core Knowledge Web Site

http://www.coreknowledge.org/
Site dedicated to providing resources for parents; based on the books of E. D. Hirsch, Jr., who wrote the *What Your X Grader Needs to Know* series.

Family Education Network

http://www.familyeducation.com/article/0,1120, 1-6219,00.html
This report presents some of the arguments against current standardized testing practices in the public schools. The site also provides links to family activities that help kids learn.

Math.com

http://www.math.com/students/testprep.html
Get ready for standardized tests.

Standardized Tests

http://arc.missouri.edu/k12/
K through 12 assessment tools and know-how.

Parents: Testing in Schools

KidSource: Talking to Your Child's Teacher about Standardized Tests

http://www.kidsource.com/kidsource/content2/ talking.assessment.k12.4.html
This site provides basic information to help parents understand their children's test results and provides pointers for how to discuss the results with their children's teachers.

eSCORE.com: State Test and Education Standards

http://www.eSCORE.com
Find out if your child meets the necessary requirements for your local schools. A Web site with experts from Brazelton Institute and Harvard's Project Zero.

Overview of States' Assessment Programs

http://ericae.net/faqs/

Parent Soup
Education Central: Standardized Tests

http://www.parentsoup.com/edcentral/testing
A parent's guide to standardized testing in the schools, written from a parent advocacy standpoint.

National Center for Fair and Open Testing, Inc. (FairTest)

342 Broadway
Cambridge, MA 02139
(617) 864-4810
http://www.fairtest.org

National Parent Information Network

http://npin.org

Publications for Parents from the U.S. Department of Education

http://www.ed.gov/pubs/parents/
An ever-changing list of information for parents available from the U.S. Department of Education.

State of the States Report

http://www.edweek.org/sreports/qc99/states/ indicators/in-intro.htm
A report on testing and achievement in the 50 states.

Testing: General Information

Academic Center for Excellence

http://www.acekids.com

American Association for Higher Education Assessment

http://www.aahe.org/assessment/web.htm

American Educational Research Association (AERA)

http://aera.net
An excellent link to reports on American education, including reports on the controversy over standardized testing.

American Federation of Teachers

555 New Jersey Avenue, NW
Washington, D.C. 20011

Association of Test Publishers Member Products and Services
http://www.testpublishers.org/memserv.htm

Education Week on the Web
http://www.edweek.org

ERIC Clearinghouse on Assessment and Evaluation
1131 Shriver Lab
University of Maryland
College Park, MD 20742
http://ericae.net
A clearinghouse of information on assessment and education reform.

FairTest: The National Center for Fair and Open Testing
http://fairtest.org/facts/ntfact.htm
http://fairtest.org/
The National Center for Fair and Open Testing is an advocacy organization working to end the abuses, misuses, and flaws of standardized testing and to ensure that evaluation of students and workers is fair, open, and educationally sound. This site provides many links to fact sheets, opinion papers, and other sources of information about testing.

National Congress of Parents and Teachers
700 North Rush Street
Chicago, Illinois 60611

National Education Association
1201 16th Street, NW
Washington, DC 20036

National School Boards Association
http://www.nsba.org
A good source for information on all aspects of public education, including standardized testing.

Testing Our Children: A Report Card on State Assessment Systems
http://www.fairtest.org/states/survey.htm
Report of testing practices of the states, with graphical links to the states and a critique of fair testing practices in each state.

Trends in Statewide Student Assessment Programs: A Graphical Summary
http://www.ccsso.org/survey96.html
Results of annual survey of states' departments of public instruction regarding their testing practices.

U.S. Department of Education
http://www.ed.gov/

Web Links for Parents Who Want to Help Their Children Achieve
http://www.liveandlearn.com/learn.html
This page offers many Web links to free and for-sale information and materials for parents who want to help their children do well in school. Titles include such free offerings as the Online Colors Game and questionnaires to determine whether your child is ready for school.

What Should Parents Know about Standardized Testing in the Schools?
http://www.rusd.k12.ca.us/parents/standard.html
An online brochure about standardized testing in the schools, with advice regarding how to become an effective advocate for your child.

Test Publishers Online

ACT: Information for Life's Transitions
http://www.act.org

American Guidance Service, Inc.
http://www.agsnet.com

Ballard & Tighe Publishers
http://www.ballard-tighe.com

Consulting Psychologists Press
http://www.cpp-db.com

CTB McGraw-Hill
http://www.ctb.com

Educational Records Bureau
http://www.erbtest.org/index.html

Educational Testing Service
http://www.ets.org

General Educational Development (GED) Testing Service
http://www.acenet.edu/calec/ged/home.html

Harcourt Brace Educational Measurement
http://www.hbem.com

Piney Mountain Press—A Cyber-Center for Career and Applied Learning
http://www.pineymountain.com

ProEd Publishing
http://www.proedinc.com

Riverside Publishing Company
http://www.hmco.com/hmco/riverside

Stoelting Co.
http://www.stoeltingco.com

Sylvan Learning Systems, Inc.
http://www.educate.com

Touchstone Applied Science Associates, Inc. (TASA)
http://www.tasa.com

Tests Online

(*Note:* We don't endorse tests; some may not have technical documentation. Evaluate the quality of any testing program before making decisions based on its use.)

Edutest, Inc.
http://www.edutest.com
Edutest is an Internet-accessible testing service that offers criterion-referenced tests for elementary school students, based upon the standards for K through 12 learning and achievement in the states of Virginia, California, and Florida.

Virtual Knowledge
http://www.smarterkids.com
This commercial service, which enjoys a formal partnership with Sylvan Learning Centers, offers a line of skills assessments for preschool through grade 9 for use in the classroom or the home. For free online sample tests, see the Virtual Test Center.

Read More about It

Abbamont, Gary W. *Test Smart: Ready-to-Use Test-Taking Strategies and Activities for Grades 5–12. Upper Saddle River,* NJ: Prentice Hall Direct, 1997.

Cookson, Peter W., and Joshua Halberstam. *A Parent's Guide to Standardized Tests in School: How to Improve Your Child's Chances for Success.* New York: Learning Express, 1998.

Frank, Steven, and Stephen Frank. *Test-Taking Secrets: Study Better, Test Smarter, and Get Great Grades (The Backpack Study Series).* Holbrook, MA: Adams Media Corporation, 1998.

Gilbert, Sara Dulaney. *How to Do Your Best on Tests: A Survival Guide.* New York: Beech Tree Books, 1998.

Gruber, Gary. *Dr. Gary Gruber's Essential Guide to Test-Taking for Kids, Grades 3–5.* New York: William Morrow & Co., 1986.

———. *Gary Gruber's Essential Guide to Test-Taking for Kids, Grades 6, 7, 8, 9.* New York: William Morrow & Co., 1997.

Leonhardt, Mary. *99 Ways to Get Kids to Love Reading and 100 Books They'll Love.* New York: Crown, 1997.

———. *Parents Who Love Reading, Kids Who Don't: How It Happens and What You Can Do about It.* New York: Crown, 1995.

McGrath, Barbara B. *The Baseball Counting Book.* Watertown, MA: Charlesbridge, 1999.

———. *More M&M's Brand Chocolate Candies Math.* Watertown, MA: Charlesbridge, 1998.

Mokros, Janice R. *Beyond Facts & Flashcards: Exploring Math with Your Kids.* Portsmouth, NH: Heinemann, 1996.

Romain, Trevor, and Elizabeth Verdick. *True or False?: Tests Stink!* Minneapolis: Free Spirit Publishing Co., 1999.

Schartz, Eugene M. *How to Double Your Child's Grades in School: Build Brilliance and Leadership into Your Child—from Kindergarten to College—in Just 5 Minutes a Day.* New York: Barnes & Noble, 1999.

Taylor, Kathe, and Sherry Walton. *Children at the Center: A Workshop Approach to Standardized Test Preparation, K–8.* Portsmouth, NH: Heinemann, 1998.

Tobia, Sheila. *Overcoming Math Anxiety.* New York: W. W. Norton & Company, Inc., 1995.

Tufariello, Ann Hunt. *Up Your Grades: Proven Strategies for Academic Success.* Lincolnwood, IL: VGM Career Horizons, 1996.

Vorderman, Carol. *How Math Works.* Pleasantville, NY: Reader's Digest Association, Inc., 1996.

Zahler, Kathy A. *50 Simple Things You Can Do to Raise a Child Who Loves to Read.* New York: IDG Books, 1997.

What Your Child's Test Scores Mean

Several weeks or months after your child has taken standardized tests, you will receive a report such as the TerraNova Home Report found in Figures 1 and 2. You will receive similar reports if your child has taken other tests. We briefly examine what information the reports include.

Look at the first page of the Home Report. Note that the chart provides labeled bars showing the child's performance. Each bar is labeled with the child's National Percentile for that skill area. When you know how to interpret them, national percentiles can be the most useful scores you encounter on reports such as this. Even when you are confronted with different tests that use different scale scores, you can always interpret percentiles the same way, regardless of the test. A percentile tells the percent of students who score at or below that level. A percentile of 25, for example, means that 25 percent of children taking the test scored at or below that score. (It also means that 75 percent of students scored above that score.) Note that the average is always at the 50th percentile.

On the right side of the graph on the first page of the report, the publisher has designated the ranges of scores that constitute average, above average, and below average. You can also use this slightly more precise key for interpreting percentiles:

PERCENTILE RANGE	LEVEL
2 and Below	Deficient
3–8	Borderline
9–23	Low Average
24–75	Average
76–97	High Average
98 and Up	Superior

The second page of the Home report provides a listing of the child's strengths and weaknesses, along with keys for mastery, partial mastery, and non-mastery of the skills. Scoring services determine these breakdowns based on the child's scores as compared with those from the national norm group.

Your child's teacher or guidance counselor will probably also receive a profile report similar to the TerraNova Individual Profile Report, shown in Figures 3 and 4. That report will be kept in your child's permanent record. The first aspect of this report to notice is that the scores are expressed both numerically and graphically.

First look at the score bands under National Percentile. Note that the scores are expressed as bands, with the actual score represented by a dot within each band. The reason we express the scores as bands is to provide an idea of the amount by which typical scores may vary for each student. That is, each band represents a

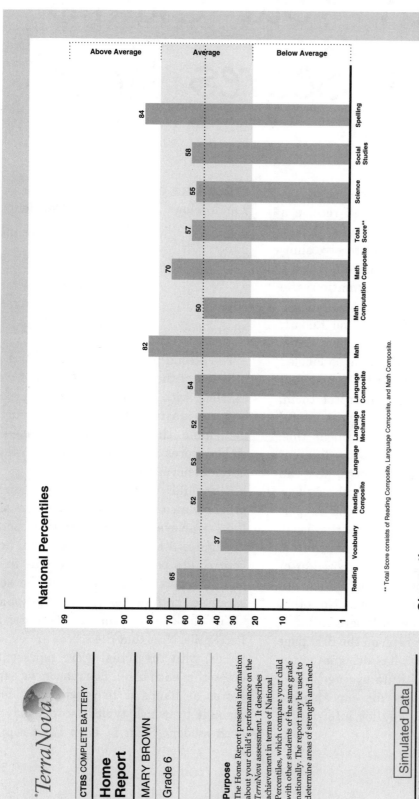

Figure 1 (SOURCE: CTB/McGraw-Hill, copyright © 1997. All rights reserved. Reproduced with permission.)

Strengths

Reading
- ● Basic Understanding
- ● Analyze Text

Vocabulary
- ● Word Meaning
- ● Words in Context

Language
- ● Editing Skills
- ● Sentence Structure

Language Mechanics
- ● Sentences, Phrases, Clauses

Mathematics
- ● Computation and Numerical Estimation
- ● Operation Concepts

Mathematics Computation
- ● Add Whole Numbers
- ● Multiply Whole Numbers

Science
- ● Life Science
- ● Inquiry Skills

Social Studies
- ● Geographic Perspectives
- ● Economic Perspectives

Spelling
- ● Vowels
- ● Consonants

Key ● Mastery

General Interpretation

The left column shows your child's best areas of performance. In each case, your child has reached mastery level. The column at the right shows the areas within each test section where your child's scores are the lowest. In these cases, your child has not reached mastery level, although he or she may have reached partial mastery.

Needs

Reading
- ◐ Evaluate and Extend Meaning
- ○ Identify Reading Strategies

Vocabulary
- ○ Multimeaning Words

Language
- ◐ Writing Strategies

Language Mechanics
- ○ Writing Conventions

Mathematics
- ◐ Measurement
- ○ Geometry and Spatial Sense

Mathematics Computation
- ○ Percents

Science
- ○ Earth and Space Science

Social Studies
- ◐ Historical and Cultural Perspectives

Spelling

No area of needs were identified for this content area

Key ◐ Partial Mastery ○ Non-Mastery

TerraNova

CTBS COMPLETE BATTERY

Home Report

MARY BROWN

Grade 6

Purpose

This page of the Home Report presents information about your child's strengths and needs. This information is provided to help you monitor your child's academic growth.

Simulated Data

Birthdate: 02/08/85
Special Codes:
A B C D E F G H I J K L M N O P Q R S T
3 5 9 7 3 2   1 1 1
Form/Level: A-16

Test Date: 11/01/99 Scoring: PATTERN (IRT)
QM: 08 Norms Date: 1996

Class: PARKER
School: WINFIELD
District: WINFIELD

City/State: WINFIELD, CA

CTB McGraw-Hill

Page 2

Figure 2 (SOURCE: CTB/McGraw-Hill, copyright © 1997. All rights reserved. Reproduced with permission.)

°TerraNova

MULTIPLE ASSESSMENTS

Individual Profile Report

MARY BROWN

Grade 7

Purpose

This report provides a comprehensive record of this student's achievement. It is a source of information for instructional planning specific to the student and a point of reference for the teacher during a parent-teacher conference. It can contribute to the student's cumulative record.

Simulated Data

Birthdate: 09/11/82
Special Codes:
A B C D E F G H I J K L M N O P Q R S T
4 0 2 2 6   1 2 1
Form/Level: A-17

Test Date: 11/01/99   Scoring: PATTERN (IRT)
QM: 07   Norms Date: 1996

Class: PARKER
School: WINFIELD
District: WINFIELD

City/State: WINFIELD, CA

CTB
McGraw-Hill   *Page 1*

CTBID:92123B82146000-04-00052-000054
W1 2PR1 P1 final:11/16

Norm-Referenced Scores

	Scale Score	Grade Equivalent	National Stanine	National Percentile	NP Range	
Reading	677	8.8	6	65	55-75	
Language	657	7.3	5	53	43-60	
Mathematics	699	9.8	7	82	74-89	
Total Score**	681	8.8	6	72	60-81	
Science	671	7.4	5	55	45-66	
Social Studies	669	7.7	5	58	48-68	

** Total Score consists of Reading, Language, and Mathematics.

National Percentile — Below Average | Average | Above Average

National Stanine

Performance on Objectives

Obj. No.	Objective Titles	Mastery Level	OPI
	Reading		
02	Basic Understanding	●	91
03	Analyze Text	●	92
04	Evaluate & Extend Meaning	◐	65
05	Identify Reading Strategies	●	70
	Language		
07	Sentence Structure	◐	63
08	Writing Strategies	◐	59
09	Editing Skills	●	78
	Mathematics		
10	Number & Number Relations	●	71
11	Comp. & Numerical Estimation	●	83
13	Measurement	◐	66
14	Geometry & Spatial Sense	●	71
15	Data Analysis, Stat. & Probability	◐	61
16	Patterns, Functions, Algebra	●	77
17	Problem Solving & Reasoning	◐	71
18	Communication	◐	69
	Science		
19	Science Inquiry	○	47
20	Physical Science	○	49
21	Life Science	○	46
22	Earth & Space Science	◐	52
23	Science & Technology	○	48
24	Personal & Social Persp.	◐	52

Obj. No.	Objective Titles	Mastery Level	OPI
	Social Studies		
26	Geographic Perspectives	●	75
27	Historical & Cultural Perspectives	◐	65
28	Civics & Government Perspectives	◐	72
29	Economic Perspectives	◐	61

Objectives Performance Index (OPI)
○ Non-Mastery   ◐ Partial Mastery   ● Mastery

Observations

Norm-Referenced Scores

The top section of the report presents information about this student's achievement in several different ways. The National Percentile (NP) data and graph indicate how this student performed compared to students of the same grade nationally. The National Percentile range indicates that if this student had taken the test numerous times the scores would have fallen within the range shown. The shaded area on the graph represents the average range of scores, usually defined as the middle 50 percent of students nationally. Scores in the area to the right of the shading are above the average range. Scores in the area to the left of the shading are below the average range.

In Reading, for example, this student achieved a National Percentile rank of 65. This student scored higher than 65 percent of the students nationally. This score is in the average range. This student has a total of five scores in the average range. One score is in the above average range. No scores are in the below average range.

Performance on Objectives

The next section of the report presents performance on the objectives. Each objective is measured by a minimum of 4 items. The Objectives Performance Index (OPI) provides an estimate of the number of items that a student could be expected to answer correctly if there had been 100 items for that objective. The OPI is used to indicate mastery of each objective. An OPI of 75 and above characterizes Mastery. An OPI between 50 and 74 indicates Partial Mastery, and an OPI below 50 indicates Non-Mastery. The two-digit number preceding the objective title identifies the objective, which is fully described in the Teacher's Guide to *TerraNova*. The bands on either side of the diamonds indicate the range within which the student's test scores would fall if the student were tested numerous times.

In Reading, for example, this student could be expected to respond correctly to 91 out of 100 items measuring Basic Understanding. If this student had taken the test numerous times the OPI for this objective would have fallen between 82 and 93.

Teacher Notes

_____

_____

_____

_____

_____

_____

_____

TerraNova

MULTIPLE ASSESSMENTS

Individual Profile Report

MARY BROWN

Grade 7

Purpose

The Observations section of the Individual Profile Report gives teachers and parents information to interpret this report. This page is a narrative description of the data on the other side.

Simulated Data

Birthdate: 09/11/82
Special Codes:
A B C D E F G H I J K L M N O P Q R S T
4 0 2 2 6   1 2 1
Form/Level: A-17
Test Date: 11/01/99   Scoring: PATTERN (IRT)
QM: 08   Norms Date: 1996

Class: PARKER
School: WINFIELD
District: WINFIELD

City/State: WINFIELD, CA

CTB
McGraw-Hill

Page 2

Figure 4 (SOURCE: CTB/McGraw-Hill, copyright © 1997. All rights reserved. Reproduced with permission.)

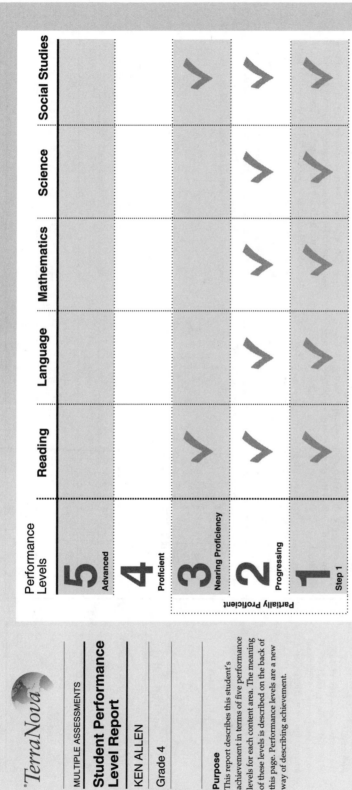

TerraNova

MULTIPLE ASSESSMENTS

Student Performance Level Report

KEN ALLEN

Grade 4

Purpose

This report describes this student's achievement in terms of five performance levels for each content area. The meaning of these levels is described on the back of this page. Performance levels are a new way of describing achievement.

| Simulated Data |

Birthdate: 02/08/86
Special Codes:
A B C D E F G H I J K L M N O P Q R S T
3 5 9 7 3 2   1 1 1
Form/Level: A-14
Test Date: 04/15/97   Scoring: PATTERN (IRT)
QM: 31   Norms Date: 1996

Class: SCHWARZ
School: WINFIELD
District: GREEN VALLEY

City/State: WINFIELD, CA

CTB
McGraw-Hill   *Page 1*

Performance Levels

Performance Levels	Reading	Language	Mathematics	Science	Social Studies
5 Advanced					
4 Proficient					
3 Nearing Proficiency	✓	✓	✓	✓	✓
2 Progressing	✓	✓	✓	✓	✓
1 Step 1	✓	✓	✓	✓	✓

Partially Proficient

Observations

Performance level scores provide a measure of what students *can do* in terms of the content and skills assessed by *TerraNova*, and typically found in curricula for Grades 3, 4, and 5. It is desirable to work towards achieving a Level 4 (Proficient) or Level 5 (Advanced) by the end of Grade 5.

The number of check marks indicates the performance level this student reached in each content area. For example, this student reached Level 3 in Reading and Social Studies.

The performance level indicates this student can perform the majority of what is described for that level and even more of what is described for the levels below. The student may also be capable of performing some of the things described in the next higher level, but not enough to have reached that level of performance.

For example, this student can perform the majority of what is described for Level 3 in Reading and even more of what is described for Level 2 and Level 1 in Reading. This student may also be capable of performing some of what is described for Level 4 in Reading.

For each content area look at the skills and knowledge described in the next higher level. These are the competencies this student needs to demonstrate to show academic growth.

Performance Levels (Grades 3, 4, 5)	Reading	Language	Mathematics	Science	Social Studies
5 Advanced	Students use analogies to generalize. They identify a paraphrase of concepts or ideas in texts. They can indicate thought processes that led them to a previous answer. In written responses, they demonstrate understanding of an implied theme, assess intent of passage information, and provide justification as well as support for their answers.	Students understand logical development in paragraph structure. They identify essential information from notes. They recognize the effect of prepositional phrases on subject-verb agreement. They find and correct at least 4 out of 6 errors when editing simple narratives. They correct run-on and incomplete sentences in more complex texts. They can eliminate all errors when editing their own work.	Students locate decimals on a number line; compute with decimals and fractions; read scale drawings; find areas; identify geometric transformations; construct and label bar graphs; find simple probabilities; find averages; use patterns in data to solve problems; use multiple strategies and concepts to solve unfamiliar problems; express mathematical ideas and explain the problem-solving process.	Students understand a broad range of grade level scientific concepts, such as the structure of Earth and instinctive behavior. They know terminology, such as decomposers, fossil fuel, eclipse, and buoyancy. Knowledge of more complex environmental issues includes, for example, the positive consequences of a forest fire. Students can process and interpret more detailed tables and graphs. They can suggest improvements to experimental design, such as running more trials.	Students consistently demonstrate skills such as synthesizing information from two sources (e.g., a document and a map). They show understanding of the democratic process and global environmental issues, and know the location of continents and major countries. They analyze and summarize information from multiple sources in early American history. They thoroughly explain both sides of an issue and give complete and detailed written answers to questions.
4 Proficient	Students interpret figures of speech. They recognize paraphrase of text information and retrieve information to complete forms. In more complex texts, they identify themes, main ideas, or author purpose/point of view. They analyze and apply information in graphic and text form, make reasonable generalizations, and draw conclusions. In written responses, they can identify key elements from text.	Students select the best supporting sentences for a topic sentence. They use compound predicates to combine sentences. They identify simple subjects and predicates, recognize correct usage when confronted with two types of errors, and find and correct at least 3 out of 6 errors when editing simple narratives. They can edit their own work with only minor errors.	Students compare, order, and round whole numbers; know place value to thousands; identify fractions; use computation and estimation strategies; relate multiplication to addition; measure to nearest half-inch and centimeter; measure and find perimeters; estimate measures; find elapsed times; combine and subdivide shapes; identify parallel lines; interpret tables and graphs; solve two-step problems.	Students have a range of specific science knowledge, including details about animal adaptations and classification, states of matter, and the geology of Earth. They recognize scientific words such as habitat, gravity, and mass. They understand the usefulness of computers. They understand reasons for conserving natural resources. Understanding of experimentation includes analyzing purpose, interpreting data, and selecting tools to gather data.	Students demonstrate skills such as making inferences, using historical documents and analyzing maps to determine the economic strengths of a region. They understand the function of currency in various cultures and supply and demand. They summarize information from multiple sources, recognize relationships, determine relevance of information, and show global awareness. They propose solutions to real-world problems and support ideas with appropriate details.
3 Nearing Proficiency (Partially Proficient)	Students use context clues and structural analysis to determine word meaning. They recognize homonyms and antonyms in grade-level text. They identify important details, sequence, cause and effect, and lessons embedded in the text. They interpret characters' feelings and apply information to new situations. In written responses, they can express an opinion and support it.	Students identify irrelevant sentences in paragraphs and select the best place to insert new information. They recognize faulty sentence construction. They can combine simple sentences with conjunctions and use simple subordination of phrases/clauses. They identify reference sources. They recognize correct conventions for dates, closings, and place names in informal correspondence.	Students identify even and odd numbers; subtract whole numbers with regrouping; multiply and divide by one-digit numbers; identify simple fractions; measure with ruler to nearest inch; tell time to nearest fifteen minutes; recognize and classify common shapes; recognize symmetry; subdivide shapes; complete bar graphs; extend numerical and geometric patterns; apply simple logical reasoning.	Students are familiar with the life cycles of plants and animals. They can identify an example of a cold-blooded animal. They infer what once existed from fossil evidence. They recognize the term habitat. They understand the water cycle. They know science and society issues such as recycling and sources of pollution. They can sequence technological advances. They extrapolate data, devise a simple classification scheme, and determine the purpose of a simple experiment.	Students demonstrate skills in organizing information. They use time lines, product and global maps, and cardinal directions. They understand simple cause and effect relationships and historical documents. They sequence events, associate holidays with events, and classify natural resources. They compare life in different times and understand some economic concepts related to products, jobs, and the environment. They give some detail in written responses.
2 Progressing (Partially Proficient)	Students identify synonyms for grade-level words, and use context clues to define common words. They make simple inferences and predictions based on text. They identify characters' feelings. They can transfer information from text to graphic form, or from graphic form to text. In written responses, they can provide limited support for their answers.	Students identify the use of correct verb tenses and supply verbs to complete sentences. They complete paragraphs by selecting an appropriate topic sentence. They select correct adjective forms.	Students know ordinal numbers; solve coin combination problems; count by tens; add whole numbers with regrouping; have basic estimation skills; understand addition property of zero; write and identify number sentences describing simple situations; read calendars; identify appropriate measurement tools; recognize congruent figures; use simple coordinate grids; read common tables and graphs.	Students recognize that plants decompose and become part of soil. They can classify a plant as a vegetable. They recognize that camouflage relates to survival. They recognize terms such as hibernate. They have an understanding of human impact on the environment and are familiar with causes of pollution. They find the correct bar graph to represent given data and transfer data appropriate for middle elementary grades to a bar graph.	Students demonstrate simple information-processing skills such as using basic maps and keys. They recognize simple geographical terms, types of jobs, modes of transportation, and natural resources. They connect a human need with an appropriate community service. They identify some early famous presidents and know the capital of the United States. Their written answers are partially complete.
1 Step 1 (Partially Proficient)	Students select pictured representations of ideas and identify stated details contained in simple texts. In written responses, they can select and transfer information from charts.	Students supply subjects to complete sentences. They identify the correct use of pronouns. They edit for the correct use of end marks and initial capital letters, and identify the correct convention for greetings in letters.	Students read and recognize numbers to 1000; identify real-world use of numbers; add and subtract two-digit numbers without regrouping; identify addition situations; recognize and complete simple geometric and numerical patterns.	Students recognize basic adaptations for living in the water, identify an animal that is hatched from an egg, and associate an organism with its correct environment. They identify an object as metal. They have some understanding of conditions on the moon. They supply one way a computer can be useful. They associate an instrument like a telescope with a field of study.	Students are developing fundamental social studies skills such as locating and classifying basic information. They locate information in pictures and read and complete simple bar graphs related to social studies concepts and contexts. They can connect some city buildings with their functions and recognize certain historical objects.

IMPORTANT: Each performance level, depicted on the other side, indicates the student can perform the majority of what is described for that level and even more of what is described for the levels below. The student may also be capable of performing some of the things described in the next higher level, but not enough to have reached that level.

W1 SPLR P2:11/02

Figure 6 (SOURCE: CTB/McGraw-Hill, copyright © 1997. All rights reserved. Reproduced with permission.)

confidence interval. In these reports, we usually report either a 90 percent or 95 percent confidence interval. Interpret a confidence interval this way: Suppose we report a 90 percent confidence interval of 25 to 37. This means we estimate that, if the child took the test multiple times, we would expect that child's score to be in the 25 to 37 range 90 percent of the time.

Now look under the section titled Norm-Referenced Scores on the first page of the Individual Profile Report (Figure 3). The farthest column on the right provides the NP Range, which is the National Percentile scores represented by the score bands in the chart.

Next notice the column labeled Grade Equivalent. Theoretically, grade level equivalents equate a student's score in a skill area with the average grade placement of children who made the same score. Many psychologists and test developers would prefer that we stopped reporting grade equivalents, because they can be grossly misleading. For example, the average reading grade level of high school seniors as reported by one of the more popular tests is the eighth grade level. Does that mean that the nation's high school seniors cannot read? No. The way the test publisher calculated grade equivalents was to determine the average test scores for students in grades 4 to 6 and then simply extend the resulting prediction formula to grades 7 to 12. The result is that parents of average high school seniors who take the test in question would mistakenly believe that their seniors are reading four grade levels behind! Stick to the percentile in interpreting your child's scores.

Now look at the columns labeled Scale Score and National Stanine. These are two of a group of scores we also call *standard scores.* In reports for other tests, you may see other standard scores reported, such as Normal Curve Equivalents (NCEs), Z-Scores, and T-Scores. The IQ that we report on intelligence tests, for example, is a standard score. Standard scores are simply a way of expressing a student's scores in terms of the statistical properties of the scores from the norm group against which we are comparing the child. Although most psychologists prefer to speak in terms of standard scores among themselves, parents are advised to stick to percentiles in interpreting your child's performance.

Now look at the section of the report labeled Performance on Objectives. In this section, the test publisher reports how your child did on the various skills that make up each skills area. Note that the scores on each objective are expressed as a percentile band, and you are again told whether your child's score constitutes mastery, non-mastery, or partial mastery. Note that these scores are made up of tallies of sometimes small numbers of test items taken from sections such as Reading or Math. Because they are calculated from a much smaller number of scores than the main scales are (for example, Sentence Comprehension is made up of fewer items than overall Reading), their scores are less reliable than those of the main scales.

Now look at the second page of the Individual Profile Report (Figure 4). Here the test publisher provides a narrative summary of how the child did on the test. These summaries are computer-generated according to rules provided by the publisher. Note that the results descriptions are more general than those on the previous three report pages. But they allow the teacher to form a general picture of which students are performing at what general skill levels.

Finally, your child's guidance counselor may receive a summary report such as the TerraNova Student Performance Level Report. (See Figures 5 and 6.) In this report, the publisher explains to school personnel what skills the test assessed and generally how proficiently the child tested under each skill.

Which States Require Which Tests

Tables 1 through 3 summarize standardized testing practices in the 50 states and the District of Columbia. This information is constantly changing; the information presented here was accurate as of the date of printing of this book. Many states have changed their testing practices in response to revised accountability legislation, while others have changed the tests they use.

Table 1   State Web Sites: Education and Testing

STATE	GENERAL WEB SITE	STATE TESTING WEB SITE
Alabama	http://www.alsde.edu/	http://www.fairtest.org/states/al.htm
Alaska	www.educ.state.ak.us/	http://www.eed.state.ak.us/tls/Performance Standards/
Arizona	http://www.ade.state.az.us/	http://www.ade.state.az.us/standards/
Arkansas	http://arkedu.k12.ar.us/	http://www.fairtest.org/states/ar.htm
California	http://goldmine.cde.ca.gov/	http://ww.cde.ca.gov/cilbranch/sca/
Colorado	http://www.cde.state.co.us/index_home.htm	http://www.cde.state.co.us/index_assess.htm
Connecticut	http://www.state.ct.us/sde	http://www.state.ct.us/sde/cmt/index.htm
Delaware	http://www.doe.state.de.us/	http://www.doe.state.de.us/aab/index.htm
District of Columbia	http://www.k12.dc.us/dcps/home.html	http://www.k12.dc.us/dcps/data/data_frame2.html
Florida	http://www.firn.edu/doe/	http://www.firn.edu/doe/sas/sasshome.htm
Georgia	http://www.doe.k12.ga.us/	http://www.doe.k12.ga.us/sla/ret/recotest.html
Hawaii	http://kalama.doe.hawaii.edu/upena/	http://www.fairtest.org/states/hi.htm
Idaho	http://www.sde.state.id.us/Dept/	http://www.sde.state.id.us/instruct/ schoolaccount/statetesting.htm
Illinois	http://www.isbe.state.il.us/	http://www.isbe.state.il.us/isat/
Indiana	http://doe.state.in.us/	http://doe.state.in.us/assessment/welcome.html
Iowa	http://www.state.ia.us/educate/index.html	(Tests Chosen Locally)
Kansas	http://www.ksbe.state.ks.us/	http://www.ksbe.state.ks.us/assessment/
Kentucky	htp://www.kde.state.ky.us/	http://www.kde.state.ky.us/oaa/
Louisiana	http://www.doe.state.la.us/DOE/asps/home.asp	http://www.doe.state.la.us/DOE/asps/home.asp? I=HISTAKES
Maine	http://janus.state.me.us/education/homepage.htm	http://janus.state.me.us/education/mea/ meacompass.htm
Maryland	http://www.msde.state.md.us/	http://www.fairtest.org/states/md.htm
Massachusetts	http://www.doe.mass.edu/	http://www.doe.mass.edu/mcas/
Michigan	http://www.mde.state.mi.us/	http://www.mde.state.mi.us/off/meap/

STATE	GENERAL WEB SITE	STATE TESTING WEB SITE
Minnesota	http://www.educ.state.mn.us/	http://fairtest.org/states/mn.htm
Mississippi	http://mdek12.state.ms.us/	http://fairtest.org/states/ms.htm
Missouri	http://services.dese.state.mo.us/	http://fairtest.org/states/mo.htm
Montana	http://www.metnet.mt.gov/	http://fairtest.org/states/mt.htm
Nebraska	http://nde4.nde.state.ne.us/	http://www.edneb.org/IPS/AppAccrd/ApprAccrd.html
Nevada	http://www.nsn.k12.nv.us/nvdoe/	http://www.nsn.k12.nv.us/nvdoe/reports/TerraNova.doc
New Hampshire	http://www.state.nh.us/doe/	http://www.state.nh.us/doe/Assessment/assessme(NHEIAP).htm
New Jersey	http://ww.state.nj.us/education/	http://www.state.nj.us/njded/stass/index.html
New Mexico	http://sde.state.nm.us/	http://sde.state.nm.us/press/august30a.html
New York	http://www.nysed.gov/	http://www.emsc.nysed.gov/ciai/assess.html
North Carolina	http://www.dpi.state.nc.us/	http://www.dpi.state.nc.us/accountability/reporting/index.html
North Dakota	http://www.dpi.state.nd.us/dpi/index.htm	http://www.dpi.state.nd.us/dpi/reports/assess/assess.htm
Ohio	http://www.ode.state.oh.us/	http://www.ode.state.oh.us/ca/
Oklahoma	http://sde.state.ok.us/	http://sde.state.ok.us/acrob/testpack.pdf
Oregon	http://www.ode.state.or.us//	http://www.ode.state.or.us/assmt/index.htm
Pennsylvania	http://www.pde.psu.edu/ http://instruct.ride.ri.net/ride_home_page.html	http://www.fairtest.org/states/pa.htm
Rhode Island		
South Carolina	http://www.state.sc.us/sde/	http://www.state.sc.us/sde/reports/terranov.htm
South Dakota	http://www.state.sd.us/state/executive/deca	http://www.state.sd.us/state/executive/deca/TA/McRelReport/McRelReports.htm
Tennessee	http://www.state.tn.us/education/	http://www.state.tn.us/education/tsintro.htm
Texas	http://www.tea.state.tx.us/	http://www.tea.state.tx.us/student.assessment/
Utah	http://www.usoe.k12.ut.us/	http://www.usoe.k12.ut.us/eval.usoeeval.htm
Vermont	http://www.cit.state.vt.us/educ/	http://www.fairtest.org/states/vt.htm

STATE	GENERAL WEB SITE	STATE TESTING WEB SITE
Virginia	http://www.pen.k12.va.us/Anthology/VDOE/	http://www.pen.k12.va.us/VDOE/Assessment/home.shtml
Washington	http://www.k12.wa.us/	http://assessment.ospi.wednet.edu/
West Virginia	http://wvde.state.wv.us/	http://www.fairtest.org/states/wv.htm
Wisconsin	http://www.dpi.state.wi.us/	http://www.dpi.state.wi.us/dpi/oea/spr_kce.html
Wyoming	http://www.k12.wy.us/wdehome.html	http://www.asme.com/wycas/index.htm

Table 2 Norm-Referenced and Criterion-Referenced Tests Administered by State

STATE	NORM-REFERENCED TEST	CRITERION-REFERENCED TEST	EXIT EXAM
Alabama	Stanford Achievement Test		Alabama High School Graduation Exam
Alaska	California Achievement Test		
Arizona	Stanford Achievement Test	Arizona's Instrument to Measure Standards (AIMS)	
Arkansas	Stanford Achievement Test		
California	Stanford Achievement Test	Standardized Testing and Reporting Supplement	High School Exit Exam (HSEE)
Colorado	None	Colorado Student Assessment Program	
Connecticut		Connecticut Mastery Test	
Delaware	Stanford Achievement Test	Delaware Student Testing Program	
District of Columbia	Stanford Achievement Test		
Florida	(Locally Selected)	Florida Comprehensive Assessment Test (FCAT)	High School Competency Test (HSCT)
Georgia	Iowa Tests of Basic Skills	Criterion-Referenced Competency Tests (CRCT)	Georgia High School Graduation Tests
Hawaii	Stanford Achievement Test	Credit by Examination	Hawaii State Test of Essential Competencies
Idaho	Iowa Test of Basic Skills/ Tests of Direct Achievement and Proficiency	Writing/Mathematics Assessment	
Illinois		Illinois Standards Achievement Tests	Prairie State Achievement Examination
Indiana		Indiana Statewide Testing for Education Progress	
Iowa	(None)		
Kansas		(State-Developed Tests)	
Kentucky	Comprehensive Tests of Basic Skills	Kentucky Instructional Results Information System	
Louisiana	Iowa Tests of Basic Skills	Louisiana Educational Assessment Program	Graduate Exit Exam
Maine		Maine Educational Assessment	
Maryland		Maryland School Performance Assessment Program	
Massachusetts		Massachusetts Comprehensive Assessment System	

STATE	NORM-REFERENCED TEST	CRITERION-REFERENCED TEST	EXIT EXAM
Michigan		Michigan Educational Assessment Program	High School Test
Minnesota		Basic Standards Test	Profile of Learning
Mississippi	Iowa Test of Basic Skills	Subject Area Testing Program	Functional Literacy Examination
Missouri		Missouri Mastery and Achievement Test	
Montana	(districts' choice)		
Nebraska			
Nevada	TerraNova		Nevada High School Proficiency Examination
New Hampshire		NH Educational Improvement and Assessment Program	
New Jersey		Elementary School Proficiency Test/Early Warning Test	High School Proficiency Test
New Mexico	TerraNova		New Mexico High School Competency Exam
New York		Pupil Evaluation Program/ Preliminary Competency Test	Regents Competency Tests
North Carolina	Iowa Test of Basic Skills	NC End of Grade Test	
North Dakota	TerraNova	ND Reading, Writing Speaking, Listening, Math Test	
Ohio		Ohio Proficiency Tests	Ohio Proficiency Tests
Oklahoma	Iowa Tests of Basic Skills	Oklahoma Criterion-Referenced Tests	
Oregon		Oregon Statewide Assessment	
Pennsylvania		Pennsylvania System of School Assessment	
Rhode Island	Metropolitan Achievement Test		
South Carolina	TerraNova	Palmetto Achievement Challenge Tests	High School Exit Exam
South Dakota	Stanford Achievement Test		
Tennessee	Tennessee Comprehensive Assessment Program	Tennessee Comprehensive Assessment Program	
Texas		Texas Assessment of Academic Skills	Texas Assessment of Academic Skills
Utah	Stanford Achievement Test	Core Curriculum Testing	

STATE	NORM-REFERENCED TEST	CRITERION-REFERENCED TEST	EXIT EXAM
Vermont		New Standards Reference Exams	
Virginia	Stanford Achievement Test	Virginia Standards of Learning	Virginia Standards of Learning
Washington	Iowa Tests of Basic Skills	Washington Assessment of Student Learning	Washington Assessment of Student Learning
West Virginia	Stanford Achievement Test		
Wisconsin	TerraNova	Wisconsin Knowledge and Concepts Examinations	
Wyoming	TerraNova	Wyoming Comprehensive Assessment System	Wyoming Comprehensive Assessment System

Table 3 Standardized Test Schedules by State

STATE	KG	1	2	3	4	5	6	7	8	9	10	11	12	COMMENT
Alabama				X	X	X	X	X	X	X	X	X	X	
Alaska					X				X			X		
Arizona			X	X	X	X	X	X	X	X	X	X	X	
Arkansas					X	X		X	X		X	X	X	
California			X	X	X	X	X	X	X	X	X	X		
Colorado				X	X			X						
Connecticut					X		X		X					
Delaware				X	X	X			X		X	X		
District of Columbia		X	X	X	X	X	X	X	X	X	X			
Florida		X	X	X	X	X	X	X	X	X	X	X	X	There is no state-mandated norm-referenced testing. However, the state collects information furnished by local districts that elect to perform norm-referenced testing. The FCAT is administered to Grades 4, 8, and 10 to assess reading and Grades 5, 8, and 10 to assess math.
Georgia				X		X			X					
Hawaii				X			X		X		X			The Credit by Examination is voluntary and is given in Grade 8 in Algebra and Foreign Languages.
Idaho				X	X	X	X	X	X	X	X	X		
Illinois				X	X			X	X	X		X	X		Exit Exam failure will not disqualify students from graduation if all other requirements are met.
Indiana				X			X		X		X			
Iowa		*	*	*	*	*	*	*	*	*	*	*	*	*Iowa does not currently have a statewide testing program. Locally chosen assessments are administered to grades determined locally.
Kansas				X	X	X		X	X		X			

STATE	KG	1	2	3	4	5	6	7	8	9	10	11	12	COMMENT
Kentucky					X	X		X	X			X	X	
Louisiana				X		X	X	X		X				
Maine					X				X			X		
Maryland				X		X			X					
Massachusetts					X				X		X			
Michigan					X	X		X	X					
Minnesota				X		X			X					Testing Information from Fair Test.Org. There was no readily accessible state-sponsored site.
Mississippi					X	X	X	X	X					State's Web site refused connection; all data were obtained from FairTest.Org.
Missouri			X	X	X	X	X	X	X	X	X			
Montana					X				X			X		The State Board of Education has decided to use a single norm-referenced test statewide beginning 2000–2001 school year.
Nebraska		**	**	**	**	**	**	**	**	**	**	**	**	**Decisions regarding testing are left to the individual school districts.
Nevada					X				X					Districts choose whether and how to test with norm-referenced tests.
New Hampshire				X			X				X			
New Jersey				X	X			X	X	X	X	X		
New Mexico					X		X		X					
New York					X				X	X				Assessment program is going through major revisions.
North Carolina				X	X	X	X	X	X		X			NRT Testing selects samples of students, not all.
North Dakota					X		X		X		X			
Ohio					X		X			X			X	
Oklahoma				X		X		X	X			X		
Oregon				X		X			X		X			

STATE	KG	1	2	3	4	5	6	7	8	9	10	11	12	COMMENT
Pennsylvania						X	X		X	X		X		
Rhode Island				X	X	X		X	X	X	X			
South Carolina				X	X	X	X	X	X	X	X			
South Dakota			X		X	X			X	X		X		
Tennessee			X	X	X	X	X	X	X			X		
Texas				X	X	X	X	X	X		X			
Utah		X	X	X	X	X	X	X	X	X	X	X	X	
Vermont					X	X	X		X	X	X	X		Rated by FairTest.Org as a nearly model system for assessment.
Virginia				X	X	X	X		X	X		X		
Washington					X			X			X			
West Virginia		X	X	X	X	X	X	X	X	X	X	X		
Wisconsin					X				X		X			
Wyoming					X				X			X		

Testing Accommodations

The more testing procedures vary from one classroom or school to the next, the less we can compare the scores from one group to another. Consider a test in which the publisher recommends that three sections of the test be given in one 45-minute session per day on three consecutive days. School A follows those directions. To save time, School B gives all three sections of the test in one session lasting slightly more than two hours. We can't say that both schools followed the same testing procedures. Remember that the test publishers provide testing procedures so schools can administer the tests in as close a manner as possible to the way the tests were administered to the groups used to obtain test norms. When we compare students' scores to norms, we want to compare apples to apples, not apples to oranges.

Most schools justifiably resist making any changes in testing procedures. Informally, a teacher can make minor changes that don't alter the testing procedures, such as separating two students who talk with each other instead of paying attention to the test; letting Lisa, who is getting over an ear infection, sit closer to the front so she can hear better; or moving Jeffrey away from the window to prevent his looking out the window and daydreaming.

There are two groups of students who require more formal testing accommodations. One group of students is identified as having a disability under Section 504 of the Rehabilitation Act of 1973 (Public Law 93-112). These students face

some challenge but, with reasonable and appropriate accommodation, can take advantage of the same educational opportunities as other students. That is, they have a condition that requires some accommodation for them.

Just as schools must remove physical barriers to accommodate students with disabilities, they must make appropriate accommodations to remove other types of barriers to students' access to education. Marie is profoundly deaf, even with strong hearing aids. She does well in school with the aid of an interpreter, who signs her teacher's instructions to her and tells her teacher what Marie says in reply. An appropriate accommodation for Marie would be to provide the interpreter to sign test instructions to her, or to allow her to watch a videotape with an interpreter signing test instructions. Such a reasonable accommodation would not deviate from standard testing procedures and, in fact, would ensure that Marie received the same instructions as the other students.

If your child is considered disabled and has what is generally called a Section 504 Plan or individual accommodation plan (IAP), then the appropriate way to ask for testing accommodations is to ask for them in a meeting to discuss school accommodations under the plan. If your child is not already covered by such a plan, he or she won't qualify for one merely because you request testing accommodations.

The other group of students who may receive formal testing accommodations are those identified as handicapped under the Individuals with Disabilities Education Act (IDEA)—students with mental retardation, learning disabilities, serious emotional disturbance, orthopedic handicap, hearing or visual problems, and other handicaps defined in the law. These students have been identified under procedures governed by federal and sometimes state law, and their education is governed by a document called the Individualized Educational Program (IEP). Unless you are under a court order specifically revoking your educational rights on behalf of your child, you are a full member of the IEP team even if you and your child's other parent are divorced and the other parent has custody. Until recently, IEP teams actually had the prerogative to exclude certain handicapped students from taking standardized group testing altogether. However, today states make it more difficult to exclude students from testing.

If your child is classified as handicapped and has an IEP, the appropriate place to ask for testing accommodations is in an IEP team meeting. In fact, federal regulations require IEP teams to address testing accommodations. You have the right to call a meeting at any time. In that meeting, you will have the opportunity to present your case for the accommodations you believe are necessary. Be prepared for the other team members to resist making extreme accommodations unless you can present a very strong case. If your child is identified as handicapped and you believe that he or she should be provided special testing accommodations, contact the person at your child's school who is responsible for convening IEP meetings and request a meeting to discuss testing accommodations.

Problems arise when a request is made for accommodations that cause major departures from standard testing procedures. For example, Lynn has an identified learning disability in mathematics calculation and attends resource classes for math. Her disability is so severe that her IEP calls for her to use a calculator when performing all math problems. She fully understands math concepts, but she simply can't perform the calculations without the aid of a calculator. Now it's time for Lynn to take the school-based standardized tests, and she asks to use a calculator. In this case, since her IEP already requires her to be provided with a calculator when performing math calculations, she may be allowed a calculator during school standardized tests. However, because using a calculator constitutes a major violation of standard testing procedures, her score on all sections in which she is allowed to use a calculator will be recorded as a failure, and her results in some states will be removed from among those of other students in her school in calculating school results.

How do we determine whether a student is allowed formal accommodations in standardized school testing and what these accommodations may be? First, if your child is not already identified as either handicapped or disabled, having the child classified in either group solely to receive testing accommodations will be considered a violation of the laws governing both classifications. Second, even if your child is already classified in either group, your state's department of public instruction will provide strict guidelines for the testing accommodations schools may make. Third, even if your child is classified in either group and you are proposing testing accommodations allowed under state testing guidelines, any accommodations must still be both *reasonable* and *appropriate*. To be reasonable and appropriate, testing accommodations must relate to your child's disability and must be similar to those already in place in his or her daily educational program. If your child is always tested individually in a separate room for all tests in all subjects, then a similar practice in taking school-based standardized tests may be appropriate. But if your child has a learning disability only in mathematics calculation, requesting that all test questions be read to him or her is inappropriate because that accommodation does not relate to his identified handicap.

Glossary

Accountability The idea that a school district is held responsible for the achievement of its students. The term may also be applied to holding students responsible for a certain level of achievement in order to be promoted or to graduate.

Achievement test An assessment that measures current knowledge in one or more of the areas taught in most schools, such as reading, math, and language arts.

Aptitude test An assessment designed to predict a student's potential for learning knowledge or skills.

Content validity The extent to which a test represents the content it is designed to cover.

Criterion-referenced test A test that rates how thoroughly a student has mastered a specific skill or area of knowledge. Typically, a criterion-referenced test is subjective, and relies on someone to observe and rate student work; it doesn't allow for easy comparisons of achievement among students. Performance assessments are criterion-referenced tests. The opposite of a criterion-referenced test is a norm-referenced test.

Frequency distribution A tabulation of individual scores (or groups of scores) that shows the number of persons who obtained each score.

Generalizability The idea that the score on a test reflects what a child knows about a subject, or how well he performs the skills the test is supposed to be assessing. Generalizability requires that enough test items are administered to truly assess a student's achievement.

Grade equivalent A score on a scale developed to indicate the school grade (usually measured in months of a year) that corresponds to an average chronological age, mental age, test score, or other characteristic. A grade equivalent of 6.4 is interpreted as a score that is average for a group in the fourth month of Grade 6.

High-stakes assessment A type of standardized test that has major consequences for a student or school (such as whether a child graduates from high school or gets admitted to college).

Mean Average score of a group of scores.

Median The middle score in a set of scores ranked from smallest to largest.

National percentile Percentile score derived from the performance of a group of individuals across the nation.

Normative sample A comparison group consisting of individuals who have taken a test under standard conditions.

Norm-referenced test A standardized test that can compare scores of students in one school with a reference group (usually other students in the same grade and age, called the "norm group"). Norm-referenced tests compare the achievement of one student or the students of a school, school district, or state with the norm score.

Norms A summary of the performance of a group of individuals on which a test was standardized.

Percentile An incorrect form of the word *centile,* which is the percent of a group of scores that falls below a given score. Although the correct term is *centile,* much of the testing literature has adopted the term *percentile.*

Performance standards A level of performance on a test set by education experts.

Quartiles Points that divide the frequency distribution of scores into equal fourths.

Regression to the mean The tendency of scores in a group of scores to vary in the direction of the mean. For example: If a child has an abnormally low score on a test, she is likely to make a higher score (that is, one closer to the mean) the next time she takes the test.

Reliability The consistency with which a test measures some trait or characteristic. A measure can be reliable without being valid, but it can't be valid without being reliable.

Standard deviation A statistical measure used to describe the extent to which scores vary in a group of scores. Approximately 68 percent of scores in a group are expected to be in a range from one standard deviation below the mean to one standard deviation above the mean.

Standardized test A test that contains well-defined questions of proven validity and that produces reliable scores. Such tests are commonly paper-and-pencil exams containing multiple-choice items, true or false questions, matching exercises, or short fill-in-the-blanks items. These tests may also include performance assessment items (such as a writing sample), but assessment items cannot be completed quickly or scored reliably.

Test anxiety Anxiety that occurs in test-taking situations. Test anxiety can seriously impair individuals' ability to obtain accurate scores on a test.

Validity The extent to which a test measures the trait or characteristic it is designed to measure. Also see *reliability.*

Answer Keys for Practice Skills

Chapter 2: Word Analysis

1	B
2	A
3	C
4	B
5	A
6	A
7	C
8	D
9	B
10	C
11	B
12	A
13	B
14	D
15	C

Chapter 3: Vocabulary

Practice Skill

1	B
2	D
3	C
4	A
5	B
6	C
7	B

8	A
9	B
10	C
11	D
12	A
13	C
14	B
15	C
16	A
17	B
18	B

Word Find

out	early	down
false	enter	new
run	ugly	fast
frown	sad	dirty
short	tame	worst

Chapter 4: Reading Comprehension

1	B
2	C
3	B
4	C
5	B
6	C
7	C

8	B
9	D
10	C
11	D
12	B
13	B

Chapter 5: Language Mechanics

1	D
2	A
3	A
4	B
5	B
6	B
7	B
8	A
9	B
10	D
11	B
12	B
13	A
14	A
15	B
16	B
17	B
18	A
19	B

20	A
21	D
22	D
23	A
24	B
25	C
26	A
27	A
28	B
29	C
30	C
31	B
32	A
33	B
34	A
35	C
36	C
37	B

Chapter 6: Math Concepts

1	B
2	C
3	C
4	B
5	D
6	C
7	B

8	A		3	D		13	B		3	D
9	D		4	A		14	D		4	C
10	D		5	C		15	C		5	B
11	C		6	B		16	A		6	D
12	A		7	A		17	C		7	A
			8	C					8	B

Chapter 7:
Math Computation

Chapter 8:
Math Applications

9	D						9	A
10	B						10	D
1	B		11	A		1	C		11	A
2	C		12	D		2	A		12	C

Sample Practice Test

A Final Review

Now that you've completed all of the chapters, your child has spent many hours reviewing the basic skills typically presented in third grade and has had lots of opportunities to practice with the standardized test format. This section provides a series of sample questions that cover all the areas previously presented. This will give your child another chance to practice the skills in a way that closely resembles what he'll face during a standardized test.

When your child takes these tests at school, each section is completed without first having a review period such as you provided when you and your child worked on the practice activities presented in each chapter.

The problems presented in this section should be completed by your child from start to finish. You should not reinforce any skills in between each section. **However, completing it *from start to finish* does not mean taking the test all in one sitting.** Instead, do one section a day, making sure that your child is not completing a section on a day that is particularly filled with outside activities or with a large amount of homework. Then, when the entire final review has been completed, look at the questions your child missed, and use them as a guide for further practice.

It's important to remember that these questions, just as the sample questions included in each chapter, can't predict your child's performance on the particular standardized test given at her school. It would be impossible for one set of ques-tions to predict performance on all the standardized tests in existence. In addition, to have your child practice all possible questions that may be encountered on a test would be an overwhelming task, and not at all practical or enjoyable. However, the questions included in this sample test can offer valuable information by giving you another opportunity to see which areas of the curriculum still present some difficulty for your child.

A final important point is that all children (and grown-ups, for that matter) are better at certain things than others. Your child will make mistakes; we all do. Help your child recognize that even though some questions will be easy and others difficult, the important thing is to read the question carefully, think about all of the choices, and then decide which is likely the best. Completion of this sample test should be considered practice: a way to determine what your child knows and to find out what to practice some more.

As you continue to work with your child, it is important to remember that learning is a process that occurs over time. If your child is still having difficulty with a certain area, that area may make sense to your child next month, or maybe the month after that. Although as parents we want our children to be successful, success on standardized tests can't be measured by 100 percent accuracy on all questions. That's just not an attainable goal, due to the nature of standardized tests. Students who feel pressure to be 100 percent correct often end up showing less than they actually know. As you work through these questions, perhaps it will help your child to understand that success in school means simply working up to her potential and feeling pleased with the results she achieves.

While your child completes these questions, try to match the situation that she'll find at school. Have her work in a quiet place. Review the directions, then have her complete one section in one sitting, with no help from you, and without any interruptions. After all sections have been completed, go back and review those areas that still present some difficulty.

To the Student:

These tests will give you a chance to put the tips you have learned to work.

A few last reminders . . .

- Be sure you understand all the directions before you begin each test. You may ask the teacher questions about the directions if you do not understand them.

- Work as quickly as you can during each test.

- When you change an answer, be sure to erase your first mark completely.

- You can guess at an answer or skip difficult items and go back to them later.

- Use the tips you have learned whenever you can.

- It is OK to be a little nervous. You may even do better.

Now that you have completed the lessons in this book, you are on your way to scoring high!

STUDENT'S NAME			SCHOOL
LAST	FIRST	MI	TEACHER
			FEMALE ○ MALE ◉

BIRTHDATE

MONTH	DAY	YEAR
JAN ○	⓪ ◉	⓪
FEB ○	① ①	①
MAR ○	② ②	②
APR ◉	◉ ③	③
MAY ○	④	④
JUN ○	⑤	⑤ ⑤
JUL ○	⑥	⑥ ⑥
AUG ○	⑦	⑦ ⑦
SEP ○	⑧	⑧ ⑧
OCT ○	⑨	⑨ ⑨
NOV ○		
DEC ○		

GRADE

① ② ③ ④ ⑤ ⑥

Word Analysis and Vocabulary

1 Ⓐ Ⓑ Ⓒ Ⓓ 6 Ⓐ Ⓑ Ⓒ Ⓓ 10 Ⓐ Ⓑ Ⓒ Ⓓ 14 Ⓐ Ⓑ Ⓒ Ⓓ 18 Ⓐ Ⓑ Ⓒ Ⓓ 22 Ⓐ Ⓑ Ⓒ Ⓓ
2 Ⓐ Ⓑ Ⓒ Ⓓ 7 Ⓐ Ⓑ Ⓒ Ⓓ 11 Ⓐ Ⓑ Ⓒ Ⓓ 15 Ⓐ Ⓑ Ⓒ Ⓓ 19 Ⓐ Ⓑ Ⓒ Ⓓ 23 Ⓐ Ⓑ Ⓒ Ⓓ
3 Ⓐ Ⓑ Ⓒ Ⓓ 8 Ⓐ Ⓑ Ⓒ Ⓓ 12 Ⓐ Ⓑ Ⓒ Ⓓ 16 Ⓐ Ⓑ Ⓒ Ⓓ 20 Ⓐ Ⓑ Ⓒ Ⓓ 24 Ⓐ Ⓑ Ⓒ Ⓓ
4 Ⓐ Ⓑ Ⓒ Ⓓ 9 Ⓐ Ⓑ Ⓒ Ⓓ 13 Ⓐ Ⓑ Ⓒ Ⓓ 17 Ⓐ Ⓑ Ⓒ Ⓓ 21 Ⓐ Ⓑ Ⓒ Ⓓ 25 Ⓐ Ⓑ Ⓒ Ⓓ
5 Ⓐ Ⓑ Ⓒ Ⓓ

Reading Comprehension

1 Ⓐ Ⓑ Ⓒ Ⓓ 4 Ⓐ Ⓑ Ⓒ Ⓓ 7 Ⓐ Ⓑ Ⓒ Ⓓ 9 Ⓐ Ⓑ Ⓒ Ⓓ 11 Ⓐ Ⓑ Ⓒ Ⓓ 13 Ⓐ Ⓑ Ⓒ Ⓓ
2 Ⓐ Ⓑ Ⓒ Ⓓ 5 Ⓐ Ⓑ Ⓒ Ⓓ 8 Ⓐ Ⓑ Ⓒ Ⓓ 10 Ⓐ Ⓑ Ⓒ Ⓓ 12 Ⓐ Ⓑ Ⓒ Ⓓ 14 Ⓐ Ⓑ Ⓒ Ⓓ
3 Ⓐ Ⓑ Ⓒ Ⓓ 6 Ⓐ Ⓑ Ⓒ Ⓓ

Language Mechanics

1 Ⓐ Ⓑ Ⓒ Ⓓ 4 Ⓐ Ⓑ Ⓒ Ⓓ 7 Ⓐ Ⓑ Ⓒ Ⓓ 10 Ⓐ Ⓑ Ⓒ Ⓓ 12 Ⓐ Ⓑ Ⓒ Ⓓ 14 Ⓐ Ⓑ Ⓒ Ⓓ
2 Ⓐ Ⓑ Ⓒ Ⓓ 5 Ⓐ Ⓑ Ⓒ Ⓓ 8 Ⓐ Ⓑ Ⓒ Ⓓ 11 Ⓐ Ⓑ Ⓒ Ⓓ 13 Ⓐ Ⓑ Ⓒ Ⓓ 15 Ⓐ Ⓑ Ⓒ Ⓓ
3 Ⓐ Ⓑ Ⓒ Ⓓ 6 Ⓐ Ⓑ Ⓒ Ⓓ 9 Ⓐ Ⓑ Ⓒ Ⓓ

Math Concepts

1 Ⓐ Ⓑ Ⓒ Ⓓ 4 Ⓐ Ⓑ Ⓒ Ⓓ 6 Ⓐ Ⓑ Ⓒ Ⓓ 8 Ⓐ Ⓑ Ⓒ Ⓓ 10 Ⓐ Ⓑ Ⓒ Ⓓ 12 Ⓐ Ⓑ Ⓒ Ⓓ
2 Ⓐ Ⓑ Ⓒ Ⓓ 5 Ⓐ Ⓑ Ⓒ Ⓓ 7 Ⓐ Ⓑ Ⓒ Ⓓ 9 Ⓐ Ⓑ Ⓒ Ⓓ 11 Ⓐ Ⓑ Ⓒ Ⓓ 13 Ⓐ Ⓑ Ⓒ Ⓓ
3 Ⓐ Ⓑ Ⓒ Ⓓ

Math Computation

1 Ⓐ Ⓑ Ⓒ Ⓓ 4 Ⓐ Ⓑ Ⓒ Ⓓ 7 Ⓐ Ⓑ Ⓒ Ⓓ 10 Ⓐ Ⓑ Ⓒ Ⓓ 13 Ⓐ Ⓑ Ⓒ Ⓓ 16 Ⓐ Ⓑ Ⓒ Ⓓ
2 Ⓐ Ⓑ Ⓒ Ⓓ 5 Ⓐ Ⓑ Ⓒ Ⓓ 8 Ⓐ Ⓑ Ⓒ Ⓓ 11 Ⓐ Ⓑ Ⓒ Ⓓ 14 Ⓐ Ⓑ Ⓒ Ⓓ 17 Ⓐ Ⓑ Ⓒ Ⓓ
3 Ⓐ Ⓑ Ⓒ Ⓓ 6 Ⓐ Ⓑ Ⓒ Ⓓ 9 Ⓐ Ⓑ Ⓒ Ⓓ 12 Ⓐ Ⓑ Ⓒ Ⓓ 15 Ⓐ Ⓑ Ⓒ Ⓓ 18 Ⓐ Ⓑ Ⓒ Ⓓ

Spelling and Punctuation

1 Ⓐ Ⓑ Ⓒ Ⓓ 4 Ⓐ Ⓑ Ⓒ Ⓓ 7 Ⓐ Ⓑ Ⓒ Ⓓ 10 Ⓐ Ⓑ Ⓒ Ⓓ 13 Ⓐ Ⓑ Ⓒ Ⓓ 16 Ⓐ Ⓑ Ⓒ Ⓓ
2 Ⓐ Ⓑ Ⓒ Ⓓ 5 Ⓐ Ⓑ Ⓒ Ⓓ 8 Ⓐ Ⓑ Ⓒ Ⓓ 11 Ⓐ Ⓑ Ⓒ Ⓓ 14 Ⓐ Ⓑ Ⓒ Ⓓ 17 Ⓐ Ⓑ Ⓒ Ⓓ
3 Ⓐ Ⓑ Ⓒ Ⓓ 6 Ⓐ Ⓑ Ⓒ Ⓓ 9 Ⓐ Ⓑ Ⓒ Ⓓ 12 Ⓐ Ⓑ Ⓒ Ⓓ 15 Ⓐ Ⓑ Ⓒ Ⓓ

WORD ANALYSIS AND VOCABULARY

Directions: Answer each question below.

1 Which word has the same vowel sound as <u>plum</u>?

  A suit

  B some

  C flute

  D out

2 Which word does not have the same vowel sound as <u>chirp</u>?

  A burn

  B fern

  C card

  D learn

3 <u>Let's</u> is the contraction for:

  A let some

  B let me

  C let his

  D let us

4 Which word has the same beginning sound as <u>goat</u>?

  A giant

  B gone

  C gentle

  D gem

5 Which word is a compound word?

  A steamboat

  B beautiful

  C happiness

  D mustard

6 Which word has the same vowel sound as <u>food</u>?

  A good

  B broom

  C hook

  D should

7 Which word has the same beginning sound as <u>single</u>?

  A cotton

  B canary

  C cupboard

  D cent

8 Which word has the same beginning sound as <u>think</u>?

  A this

  B thought

  C than

  D those

9 Which word has the same ending sound as <u>tie</u>?

  A silly

  B my

  C happy

  D funny

10 Which word has the same vowel sound as <u>cloud</u>?

  A would

  B blow

  C good

  D now

GO

11 Which word has the same vowel sound as <u>hope</u>?

A how
B mouse
C slot
D float

Directions: Choose a word or words that mean the same thing as the underlined word.

12 To <u>wander</u> is to:

A run
B jump
C walk
D skip

---

13 To <u>rattle</u> is to:

A make noise
B shake
C bite
D hold

---

14 <u>Seldom</u> means:

A a lot
B rarely
C one at a time
D quietly

---

15 A <u>collection</u> is a:

A picture
B group
C story
D toy

---

16 An <u>elephant</u> is a kind of:

A insect
B reptile
C mammal
D bird

---

17 Something is <u>harmless</u> if it:

A hurts
B is safe
C cuts
D is pretty

---

18 If something <u>disappears</u> it:

A is found
B is broken
C vanishes
D is repaired

---

19 Something is <u>helpful</u> if it:

A hurts
B doesn't help
C makes noise
D helps

---

20 To <u>repaint</u> means to:

A clean
B repair
C remove
D paint again

---

21 <u>Unpleasant</u> means:

A not pleasant
B most pleasant
C very pleasant
D fairly pleasant

GO

22 Another way to say <u>not covered</u> is:

    A discovered

    B uncovered

    C recovered

    D miscovered

23 Which words are in alphabetical order?

A	class	clown	cotton	church
B	church	clown	class	cotton
C	cotton	clown	class	church
D	church	class	clown	cotton

24 Which words are in alphabetical order?

A	splash	sparkle	spleen	splint
B	sparkle	splash	spleen	splint
C	sparkle	splash	splint	spleen
D	spleen	splash	splint	sparkle

25 Which word would NOT be on the dictionary page with these guide words?

empty	envision

    A empire

    B enter

    C enjoy

    D envelope

STOP

READING COMPREHENSION

Directions: Read the following short story and answer the questions.

Even though Jake was working on his favorite art project, he found himself looking at the clock all afternoon. Every time he looked, only a few more minutes had passed. Finally the bell rang. After he got his coat and back-pack, Jake ran home as fast as he could. He was very excited today because he had a surprise waiting for him. Today was the day Jake's new puppy was old enough to come live at his house!

As soon as Jake entered his house, he heard soft barking coming from the kitchen. After he put his backpack in his room and hung up his coat, he headed for the barking. Trying to be as careful as he could, Jake opened the kitchen door very slowly and looked around. At first he thought he saw a black ball in the middle of the puppy's new bed. But when he looked carefully, he saw two tiny ears and a little pink tongue. Jake tiptoed over and started to pet his new puppy. As soon as he did, the puppy jumped up and licked his face. Jake was very glad to be home!

1 Where was Jake at the beginning of the story?

   A   at his house
   B   at school
   C   at the library
   D   at the park

2 What did Jake do after he got his coat on?

   A   talked to the teacher
   B   played with his friends
   C   did his homework
   D   ran home

3 What color was the puppy?

   A   brown
   B   white
   C   black
   D   brown and white

4 Why did Jake look at the clock every few minutes?

   A   He was worried.
   B   He was excited.
   C   He was sad.
   D   He was bored.

5 Why did Jake open the kitchen door slowly?

   A   He didn't want to hurt the puppy.
   B   He wasn't sure the puppy was there.
   C   His mother was sleeping.
   D   The door was broken.

6 What did Jake do before he saw the puppy?

   A   Got a snack.
   B   Said hello to his mother.
   C   Put his backpack in his room.
   D   Did his homework.

Directions: Read the following short story and answer the questions.

The snow started to fall about 4:30 on Friday afternoon. Sarah was sitting at her desk, finishing her homework, when she started to get hungry. As she stood up, she happened to glance out the window. What a surprise it was to see the blanket of white across her front lawn! Even though she had four more math problems to do, Sarah decided that she would finish her homework tomorrow. She quickly put her books away and called her friend.

"Jane, have you looked outside your window yet?"

"Oh, Sarah. Let's go play. I'll meet you under your front tree."

As soon as the girls had their snow clothes on, they ran to their favorite tree. The branches hung so low to the ground that it was like a secret hiding spot. Taking care not to shake the branches too much, they slowly slithered to the tree trunk. Leaning back, they closed their eyes and listened to the snow as it fell to the ground. Sarah was surprised when she heard soft rustling above her. At first she thought it was Jane shaking one of the branches. But then she didn't see any snow coming down. When she looked up, she saw a tiny bird fixing its nest. Sarah was glad to see that the bird had a secret hiding spot too.

After a while, Jane's brother came out to find them. The girls were very careful not to make a sound when Bobby walked past. But after he went to the back of the house, they quickly left the tree and ran after him. He was already starting to build a snowman.

"What a great idea," Jane said.

Together, they made three balls of snow and found some stones for his eyes and two sticks for his arms. When they stood back to look at the snowman, Jane cried out, "Oh," and quickly ran back to the house. A few minutes later, she came back with a scarf and a big orange carrot!

7 What was the <u>blanket of white</u> across Sarah's front yard?

A clouds

B snow

C her mother's car

D an old towel

8 Why did Sarah stand up while she was doing her homework?

A She wanted to see the snow.

B She finished her homework.

C She wanted to get a snack.

D She was tired of sitting.

9 What did Sarah do before she called Jane?

A Put snow clothes on.

B Had a snack.

C Asked her mother if she could play with Jane.

D Put her books away.

10 Why didn't the girls make any noise when Jane's brother walked by?

A They didn't want to scare the bird.

B They were listening to the snow.

C They didn't want him to find their hiding spot.

D They didn't want to scare him.

11 What was Jane's brother's name?

  A John
  B Bobby
  C Jake
  D The story didn't say.

12 The best title for this story is:

  A Missing a Snack
  B No School
  C The Bird
  D A Blanket of Snow

Directions: Read the following short story. What sentence would most likely come next?

Fred's father gave him an old shoe box so he could finish his book project. When he opened the box, he was surprised to find that it was filled with old newspaper. He knew his father had forgotten that anything was in it, so he decided to clean it out carefully. When he took the last piece of newspaper out, something dropped on his foot.

13 **A** He glued the paper to the top of the box.

  B He reached down to pick up the old card.

  C He gathered the materials for his book project.

  D He threw out the newspaper.

Directions: Read the following short story. What sentence would most likely come next?

Roger hopped quickly across the ground. He was getting very hungry and had been away from the pond all day. It was fun to explore the woods around the pond, but he had to be careful that he did not go near any of the crows. They liked to scare the frogs with their big, loud flapping wings. Roger saw the pond in the distance. He could also see little bugs flying near the water's surface. His stomach started to grumble so he hopped even faster. Just then he heard a loud noise.

14 **A** Roger went to the woods to explore again.

  B Roger looked up to see a crow flying overhead.

  C Roger decided to rest.

  D Roger saw a pretty flower along the road.

STOP

LANGUAGE EXPRESSION

Directions: Read each sentence. Then choose the sentence that uses the underlined word in the same way.

1 We must <u>plant</u> the seeds in the field.

  A   My <u>plant</u> is very large and green.

  B   Sally's <u>plant</u> has many flowers on it.

  C   Put her <u>plant</u> in the backyard.

  D   I decided to <u>plant</u> flowers at my house.

2 Our class <u>play</u> is about a witch.

  A   I asked Betty to <u>play</u> with me.

  B   Did you enjoy being the lion in your <u>play</u>?

  C   Robert likes to <u>play</u> soccer.

  D   My cat and dog always <u>play</u> with their toys.

3 The soldier decided to <u>fire</u> his rifle.

  A   We must <u>fire</u> at the target when we practice.

  B   The army set up a <u>fire</u> at their camp.

  C   Make sure the <u>fire</u> doesn't get too big.

  D   Our hot <u>fire</u> made a loud crackling noise.

4 She <u>giggles</u> every time she hears a joke.

  A   We heard a lot of <u>giggles</u> from the students.

  B   His <u>giggles</u> were loud and funny.

  C   He <u>giggles</u> at the silly bird.

  D   Sally and Jane had many <u>giggles</u> together.

5 My sister has to <u>wash</u> the dishes.

  A   Did you put your clothes in the <u>wash</u>?

  B   The <u>wash</u> was finished by the time I arrived to help.

  C   Please <u>wash</u> your hands before you eat.

  D   They finished their <u>wash</u> last night.

Directions: Read each sentence. Choose the word that means the same thing as the underlined word.

6 The man was very <u>glad</u> when we gave him the balloons.

  A   happy
  B   sad
  C   worried
  D   angry

7   Her red dress was <u>beautiful</u>.

A   ugly
B   colorful
C   large
D   pretty

8   Another word for <u>find</u> is:

A   lose
B   fee
C   discover
D   wants

9   We like to <u>listen</u> to the drums and trumpets.

A   play
B   hear
C   watch
D   learn

10   Which word is NOT another word for <u>small</u>?

A   tiny
B   little
C   huge
D   wee

11   The <u>forest</u> was dark and noisy.

A   box
B   woods
C   house
D   fort

12   The boy got <u>injured</u> while he was climbing the tree.

A   scared
B   nervous
C   angry
D   hurt

13   We were all <u>silent</u> while working on our art projects.

A   quiet
B   noisy
C   happy
D   loud

14   John had to <u>repair</u> his skateboard.

A   sharpen
B   paint
C   fix
D   assemble

15   The children were <u>fearful</u> when they saw the lion.

A   happy
B   scared
C   surprised
D   excited

STOP

MATH CONCEPTS

Directions: Choose the number that belongs in the blank.

1 394 399 _____ 409

    A 304
    B 404
    C 405
    D 403

2 1586 _____ 1594 1598

    A 1588
    B 1589
    C 1590
    D 1592

3 2791 2891 2991 _____

    A 2995
    B 3901
    C 3991
    D 3091

4 What number is 1307?

    A one thousand three hundred seventy
    B one thousand thirty-seven
    C thirteen thousand, thirty-seven
    D one thousand three hundred seven

5 What is the value of the underlined number? 4<u>6</u>81

    A 60
    B 6
    C 600
    D 6000

6 What is the value of the underlined number? <u>3</u>962

    A 3000
    B 30
    C 3
    D 300

7 What is the value of the underlined number? 87<u>5</u>4

    A 5 hundreds
    B 5 tens
    C 5 thousands
    D 5 ones

8 *Five thousand twenty-nine* is what number?

    A 529
    B 5029
    C 5209
    D 5290

9 Put these numbers in order from largest to smallest:

    6403, 6078, 6199, 6412

    A 6199 6078 6412 6403
    B 6078 6199 6403 6412
    C 6412 6403 6078 6199
    D 6412 6403 6199 6078

10 What number belongs in the blank?

    $8 + 7 = 3 + \_\_\_\_$

    A 15   **B** 12
    C 11   **D** 9

GO →

11 What number belongs in the blank?

3076 < _____

A 3075
B 3173
C 3070
D 2998

12 What part of the figure below is shaded?

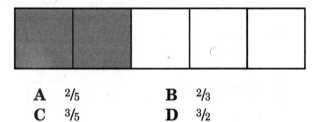

A ²/₅   **B** ²/₃
C ³/₅   **D** ³/₂

13 About how many baseball bats is the perimeter of this window?

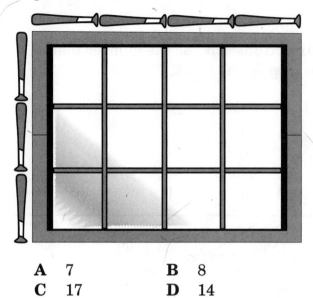

A 7   **B** 8
C 17   **D** 14

STOP

MATH COMPUTATION

Directions: Choose the correct answer for each question.

1 Laura had 329 silver coins. Sarah had 136 silver coins. How many more did Laura have than Sarah?

  A   193
  B   465
  C   213
  D   not enough information

2 There were 17 tigers, 136 elephants, and 426 zebras at the zoo. How many animals were at the zoo?

  A   732
  B   569
  C   579
  D   not enough information

3 Betty made 123 cookies for the bake sale. Katie made brownies and Laura made cupcakes. How many things in all did they make for the bake sale?

  A   123
  B   126
  C   369
  D   not enough information

4 John wanted to buy 189 pieces of bubble gum for his class. He had 121 pieces so far. How many more did he need to buy?

  A   310
  B   168
  C   68
  D   not enough information

5 Sandy found 3 pencil kits in her desk. Each pencil kit had 5 pencils in it. How many pencils did she find in all?

  A   8
  B   15
  C   2
  D   not enough information

6 Chris gave 27 football cards to his 9 friends. They all got the same amount. How many did each friend get?

  A   3
  B   16
  C   4
  D   not enough information

7 Matt had 48 pet rocks. George had 29 pet crickets. Bob had pet ladybugs. How many pets did they have in all?

  A   77
  B   21
  C   67
  D   not enough information

8 If a hot dog cost 50 cents and a soda cost 35 cents, what coins would you need?

  A   3 quarters, 1 dime
  B   2 quarters, 2 nickels
  C   4 dimes
  D   2 nickels

9 If the toy dog costs $4.20 and you gave the cashier a $5 bill, how much change would you get?

A 50 cents   **B** 10 cents

C 80 cents   **D** 25 cents

10 $1.36 is the same as:

A

B

C

D

11 George bought 4 boxes of candy. Each box had 4 large candy bars in it. How many candy bars did George have in all?

A 1

B 8

C 16

D not enough information

12 Jeff had 476 baseball cards. His friend had 193 baseball cards. How many cards did they have all together?

A 669

B 283

C 569

D not enough information

13   1376
       + 4619

A 5995

B 6096

C 6085

D 5985

14   481
       − 27

A 464

B 445

C 454

D 464

15   322
       + 164

A 487

B 158

C 486

D 487

16   581
       − 301

A 882

B 280

C 200

D 279

GO

17   473
      + 163

    A 636
    B 536
    C 310
    D 626

18   1238
      − 172

    A 1166
    B 1056
    C 1146
    D 1066

STOP

SPELLING AND PUNCTUATION

Directions: Locate the spelling or punctuation error in each sentence.

1 We must <u>buy</u> <u>apples</u> <u>oranges,</u> and <u>pears</u>.
          A   **B**   **C**   **D**

2 <u>Their</u> are 3 <u>running</u> <u>tigers</u> at the <u>zoo</u>.
  A   **B**   **C**   **D**

3 <u>Please</u> <u>don't</u> <u>right</u> in <u>your</u> book.
  A   **B**   **C**   **D**

4 I <u>new</u> that <u>our</u> class would <u>write</u> a good
    A   **B**   **C**
<u>story!</u>
  D

5 <u>do</u> you like <u>new</u> <u>blue</u> boots or old <u>red</u>
  A   **B** **C**   **D**
ones?

6 <u>Our</u> <u>new</u> <u>stares</u> are very <u>steep</u>.
  A **B** **C**   **D**

7 <u>Weed</u> like to <u>see</u> the fast <u>boat</u>, plane,
  A   **B**   **C**
and <u>car</u>.
     D

8 He was <u>too</u> <u>week</u> <u>to</u> lift the <u>heavy</u> box.
     A   **B** **C**   **D**

9 Did you <u>no</u> that <u>no</u> <u>deer</u> <u>lived</u> in the
       A   **B** **C** **D**
park?

Directions: Choose the correct way to write each sentence.

10 Mother said "Come get your breakfast."

  A Mother said, "Come get your breakfast."

  B Mother said come get your breakfast.

  C Mother said, "come get your breakfast."

  D Mother said, "Come get your breakfast"

11 Brownie is the cutest cat I've ever saw!

  A Brownie is the cuttest cat I've ever saw!

  B Brownie is the cutest cat I've ever seen!

  C Brownie is the cutest cat I've ever saw!

  D Brownie is the cutest Cat I've ever seen!

12 Sarah has three cows on his grandfather's farm.

   A Sarah has three cows on his grandfathers farm.

   B Sarah has three cowes on his grandfather's farm.

   C Sarah has three cows, on his grandfather's farm.

   D Sarah has three cows on her grandfather's farm.

13 I like to eat bananas are my favorite food.

   A I like to eat bananas. Are my favorite food.

   B I like to eat. Bananas are my favorite food.

   C I like to eat bananas, are my favorite food.

   D I like to eat Bananas are my favorite food.

14 Julie makes up new storys to tell her friends.

   A Julie makes up new storys to tell her freinds.

   B Julie makes up knew storys to tell her friends.

   C Julie makes up new stories to tell her friends.

   D Julie makes up new storys, to tell her friends.

15 She picked the rippest apples for her pie.

   A She pickked the rippest apples for her pie.

   B She picked the rippest applees for her pie.

   C She picked the rippest apples for her pye.

   D She picked the ripest apples for her pie.

16 The doctor examineed her knee after she fell off the horse.

   A The doctor examined her knee after she fell off the horse.

   B The doctor examineed her knee after she fell of the horse.

   C The doctor examineed her nee after she fell off the horse.

   D The doctor examineed her knee after she falled off the horse.

17 Bob has a job he rakes leaves for his neighbor.

   A Bob has a job he rakes leafs for his neighbor.

   B Bob has a job he rakes leaves for his nieghbor.

   C Bob has a job he rakes leaves. For his neighbor.

   D Bob has a job. He rakes leaves for his neighbor.

STOP

Answer Key for Sample Practice Test

Word Analysis and Vocabulary

1	B
2	C
3	D
4	B
5	A
6	B
7	D
8	B
9	B
10	D
11	D
12	C
13	A
14	B
15	B
16	C
17	B
18	C
19	D
20	D
21	A
22	B
23	D
24	B
25	A

Reading Comprehension

1	B
2	D
3	C
4	B
5	A
6	C
7	B
8	C
9	D
10	C
11	B
12	D
13	B
14	B

Language Expression

1	D
2	B
3	A
4	C
5	C
6	A
7	D
8	C
9	B
10	C
11	B
12	D
13	A
14	C
15	B

Math Concepts

1	B
2	C
3	D
4	D
5	C
6	A
7	B
8	B
9	D
10	B
11	B
12	A
13	D

Math Computation

1	A
2	C
3	D
4	C
5	B
6	A
7	D
8	A
9	C
10	B
11	C
12	A
13	A
14	C
15	C
16	B
17	A
18	D

Spelling and Punctuation

1	B
2	A
3	C
4	A
5	A
6	C
7	A
8	B
9	A
10	A
11	B
12	D
13	B
14	C
15	D
16	A
17	D

WORKSHEET

WORKSHEET